p 20

i.) What gift u

words are eternal p 90.
p102 Annual prophetic conference
Finished 4-24-16 one month

The Best Is Yet To Come!

Raise your head, look and see
The wonderful promise of eternity
His future for you, so near at hand
A sure, solid base, not built on sand
The footing is dug, the foundation laid
In His image you were wonderfully made
In a day so true and filled with joy
Yes the enemy came with his veiled ploy
He deceived some and they lost their way
But you've remained faithful and stood this day
You're crossing over and moving up
Eat of His flesh and drink from His cup
Look not to the past for the good or the bad
But stand, be strong, let your heart be glad
For He speaks to the North and calls to the South
To the East and West a cry comes from His mouth
Tho' many He calls, few He has chosen
Some have answered but many stand frozen
But no, not you, for you have stepped out
So choose to be chosen and don't ever doubt
He has called you, chose you, and given His Spirit
Your destiny and purpose are drawing near it
So let all know and not just some
The Father has spoken
The Best is yet to Come!

ACTIVATING THE PROPHETIC

BY

CLAY NASH

Spring Mill Publishing
Sharpsburg, Maryland USA

First Printing: 2011

ISBN: 978-0-9835857-0-1

Cover design by James Nesbit and Erik Bryson.

Editing, Text design and Typesetting by Jim Bryson.

Dedication

I dedicate this book to the memory of Bob Nash, my dad, my best friend, and an amazing voice into my life. It was because of you, Dad, that I truly learned to recognize the voice of God.

Acknowledgments

I want to thank my wonderful wife Susan, my companion and best friend. It is your belief, support and prayers that allowed me to live out this book for many years before it was written.

I also thank my children: Dawn, Diane and Dean, who are the apple of my eye and joy of my heart. You have been such a source of love and inspiration as I discovered how to hear God.

To my grandchildren: Haley, Logan, Hunter and Hannah, I pray you inherit the same grace to recognize His voice daily.

Finally, I thank the countless men and women who have pulled on the prophetic anointing, causing me to discover new depths of recognizing God's voice in exciting ways.

Jesus, thank you for allowing me to learn to "enjoy God at all times."

Table Of Contents

Foreword

It is with great excitement that I write the foreword for this book. I say this not just because Clay Nash is my friend, which he certainly is, but even more so because of its content. The Body of Christ needs this book and many more on this subject.

The prophetic realm of Kingdom life is tremendously exciting. Nothing is more thrilling than hearing God speak, whether directly or indirectly, and nothing is more fulfilling than knowing God used you to speak His word to another individual. I still remember the first prophetic word God ever used me to bring—I was euphoric for days.

At the same time, it is also true that immaturity and inaccuracy in the prophetic realm can be dangerous—so much so that there was a time in history when false prophets were stoned! All of us have heard horror stories of people hurt by prophecy, either because the word wasn't accurate or because the recipient didn't understand how to properly interpret and/or respond to it. This, of course, produces cynicism in some and bitterness in others as they throw the proverbial "baby out with the bath water."

Then there are the super-spiritual, self-proclaimed prophets roaming to and fro seeking whom they may devour! We've all met the "prophetic" person who hears from God so perfectly that no one could possibly bring any correction or discipline to them. They've "heard from God" and that's all there is to it. And what charismatic leader hasn't dealt with those who live so "out there" in the realm of seeing and hearing that they seem more in touch with "the twilight zone" than reality?

But regardless of the false, the inaccurate, the extreme and the weird, it is foolish to throw out or shy away from the prophetic. What we need is to grow in our understanding of it. For example, my daughters were not good drivers the first time they got behind the wheel of a car. None of us were. In fact, had they been released to drive on a busy highway at that point, they could have injured themselves or someone else. What was the solution? I enrolled them in a safe driving course and allowed them to drive in safe situations with their mother or me alongside. They both matured into good drivers.

This book is a "safe prophecy" course. Tried and proven prophet-teachers, such as Clay Nash, can guide us into this much needed realm of Kingdom-living with skill and accuracy. Read and study this resource. Leaders, teach it. God is calling us to rise to a new level of hearing His voice—all of us. And we can.

When the Lord was fashioning Israel into a nation, Moses gave us a look ahead into God's ultimate plan and desire as it relates to prophesy. When the Holy Spirit took of Moses' anointing and distributed it to seventy elders, some were a little jealous for Moses. Let's limit the prophesying to Moses and those close to him, was the mind-set. Moses' response epitomized what should always be the heart of a true leader: "would that all the Lord's people were prophets, that the Lord would put His Spirit upon them!" (Numbers 11:29).

Leaders who carry God's heart are always desirous to see others do what they can do—better! As we march ever so quickly toward a Third Great Awakening in America, followed by a true Reformation of society and culture, it is imperative that we hear God more clearly than ever and that we raise up a prophetic generation who knows His voice intimately. Activating the Prophetic will help us do just that.

Prayerfully read this book and glean from its teaching.

—Dutch Sheets

Dutch Sheets Ministries

Introduction

We are living in very exciting but challenging times. The Ecclesia—the Church—is changing and God is a very present help in a time of trouble. I have chosen to write in the pages of this book many of the experiences I gained living the life of a prophet of God. I want this book to create in you, the reader, a wild passion to know Him and the power of His resurrection, by recognizing His voice. The past 25+ years of ministry have convinced me that most people do not recognize God's voice, and therefore they spend much of their lives pursuing purposes not intended for them.

Since I was not raised in church, much of God's work for the first 28 years of my life was used to form who I was to become in Christ. Yes, *we know that God causes all things to work together for good to those who love God, to those who are called according to His purpose* (Romans 8:28). Since allowing Christ to become Lord and Savior, I have given my all to know Him, serve Him and love Him with abandonment. It is out of this relationship that my ability to recognize His voice has been established.

Many today seek to discover, receive, and develop a prophetic gifting. But I have discovered that a relationship with the King of the Universe gives us more than prophetic gifting, it gives us access to His way of Life. Psalm 84:5 (NASB) tells us:

> *Blessed is the man whose strength is in You, In whose heart are the highways to Zion!*

In the heart of all mankind are the highways to Zion. We were created to recognize God's voice and discover the highway to Zion, causing us to become the agents of God we were born to be.

Many people today approach the prophetic from a mystical viewpoint. In doing so, they incorrectly associate all strange and supernatural occurrences with a genuine work of Holy Spirit. This error has caused many to misunderstand God's voice and to be driven from a deep relationship where God speaks on a daily basis.

I hope my writings will cause you to press in to a deeper relationship with God the Father through Holy Spirit. There is nothing like having a living, breathing relationship with Father God where He hears you and you hear Him. My wife has said on many occasions that when you sit under my ministry, you need a good set of teeth and a strong stomach to digest what I am teaching. This being true, (of course it's true—she said it!) I pray that God's anointing will become your teacher as you read this book. My words are words of experience, not words of theory. I want you to clearly understand that this book comes from a life dedicated to recognizing God's voice and obeying it.

I have spoken, to the surprise of many, of three ways which God prefers not to speak to people; they are through circumstances, fleeces and prophets. The God of the universe, the Creator of all, wants a relationship with you. He does not want to relate to you through a third person or event. He desires to be direct. I believe He does not even desire the relationship to be based on the Bible alone. He longs to speak to you and have you speak with Him. Yes, the God of Creation has not stopped speaking. Matthew 4:4 tells us:

> But He <Jesus> answered and said, "It is written, 'Man shall not live by bread alone, but by every word that proceeds from the mouth of God.'"

Notice the word "proceeds" in this scripture was not written in past tense, but in present perfect tense. God is still speaking words from His mouth today, and those words bring faith and give life.

May this book enrich your life, build your faith, give you hope, and most of all, cause you to pursue a deeper level of *the grace of the Lord Jesus Christ, and the love of God, and the communion of the Holy Spirit be with you all...*(II Corinthians 13:14).

Chapter 1

Attributes and Personality of <the> Holy Spirit

But God has revealed himself to us through His Spirit. He searches all things. The Spirit searches all things, yea, the deep things of God. For what man knows the things of man except the spirit of the man which is in him. Even so, no one knows the things of God except the Spirit of God. We have received not the spirit of the world but the Spirit who is from God that we might know the things that have been freely given to us. (1 Corinthians 2:10-15)

When I use the term "Holy Spirit," what comes to mind? A dove? God's voice? Tongues of fire? Tongues of men and angels? A quiver in the liver? A chill in the spine? The unquenchable fire of God and the untouchable holiness of the same? Yes, He is all these things and more.

In teaching Christians to recognize the voice of God, I find it necessary to first teach them about the primary emissary of the Godhead, that of Holy Spirit. It is primarily through the ministry of Holy Spirit that man hears God. Throughout this book, I tend to use the terms "voice of God" and "voice of Holy Spirit" synonymously.

Christians hear the term "Holy Spirit" so much that we sometimes take for granted who or what Holy Spirit really is. In my 25+ years of ministry, I have had the privilege of experiencing God's Holy Spirit and ministering Him to countless believers. In my travels, however, I have encountered a surprising lack of knowledge among God's people on the true nature of this incredible companion, teacher, comforter, and guardian sent by God through the life of his son Jesus.

The first thing to understand is that Holy Spirit has his own personality and attributes. Holy Spirit is a real person. He's not simply a white cloud or a dove or tongues of fire. While these are forms which

He takes, Holy Spirit is the third person of the Godhead, which is why I refer to him as "Holy Spirit" and not *"The* Holy Spirit." It may sound funny, but think how it would sound if people called me, *"The* Clay Nash." Well, come to think of it, that does have a nice ring to it. But really, Holy Spirit is the name of a person and member of the Godhead, just like Jesus and Father, so that is how I refer to Him. He is the Spirit of God, and His name is Holy Spirit.

Scripture teaches us many aspects of Holy Spirit which the average believer may not be aware of. For example, Holy Spirit has a mind and emotions. A comprehensive study of scripture reveals the following about Holy Spirit:

1. He has knowledge.

For what man knows the things of a man except the spirit of the man which is in him? Even so no one knows the things of God except the Spirit of God. (1 Corinthians 2:11)

2. He has a will.

But one and the same Spirit works all these things, distributing to each one individually as He wills. (1 Corinthians 12:11)

3. He has a mind.

Now He who searches the hearts knows what the mind of the Spirit is, because He makes intercession for the saints according to the will of God. (Romans 8:27)

4. He loves.

Now I beg you, brethren, through the Lord Jesus Christ, and through the love of the Spirit, that you strive together with me in prayers to God for me, (Romans 15:30)

Now hope does not disappoint, because the love of God

has been poured out in our hearts by the Holy Spirit who was given to us. (Romans 5:5)

5. He searches all things.

But God has revealed them to us through His Spirit. For the Spirit searches all things, yes, the deep things of God. (1 Corinthians 2:10)

6. He teaches.

But the Helper, the Holy Spirit, whom the Father will send in My name, He will teach you all things, and bring to your remembrance all things that I said to you. (John 14:26)

7. He speaks & guides.

However, when He, the Spirit of truth, has come, He will guide you into all truth; for He will not speak on His own authority, but whatever He hears He will speak; and He will tell you things to come. (John 16:13)

So Holy Spirit is more than just the power of God or the essence of God emanating towards us. He is an independent being—a fully vested member of the Godhead. And as a being with a mind, a will, and emotions, it is understood that He will operate in those aspects of His personality. For example, scripture refers to Holy Spirit being grieved.

And do not grieve the Holy Spirit of God, by whom you were sealed for the day of redemption. (Ephesians. 4:30)

In I Thessalonians 5:19, we are told: *Do not quench the Spirit.* Obviously, Holy Spirit is a being which can be quenched or we would not be warned against it. Another way to think of quenching is "to vex, frustrate, or oppose." Acts 7:51 states it in more severe language: *You stiff-necked and uncircumcised in heart and ears! You always resist the Holy Spirit; as your fathers did, so do you.* I would hate to have that spoken to me; I can't imagine anyone who would like it.

However, the key aspect of Holy Spirit that I want to focus on for this chapter is illustrated in Hebrews 3:7: *Therefore, as the Holy Spirit says: "Today, if you will hear His voice...."* Holy Spirit has a voice. We already learned that He has a mind, emotions, a will, and requires honor. Doesn't it make sense that He would have the means to express Himself to those to whom He has been given charge for witnessing, instruction, guiding, leading, and helping.

Holy Spirit is very important in the walk of the believer. In 2 Corinthians 13:14, it says, *The grace of the Lord Jesus Christ, and the love of God, and the communion of the Holy Spirit be with you all.* The key word here is "communion." We are to commune with Holy Spirit in order to build relationship. Now, this means more than just listening with our ears or memorizing scripture or displaying supernatural signs; it means actually soaking in the Spirit of God.

When I married my wife, I thought I knew her. I knew her name—it was there on her birth certificate, so I knew where she'd come from. (Southern born and raised, praise God!) We had known each other since we were eight and talked a lot before we married. We even had pre-marriage counseling. I thought I understood this woman, head to toe, inside and out. But once we started living together as husband and wife—was I ever wrong! I never knew I had so much to learn. In the forty years I have known her, I have learned a lot, but I'm still learning this woman and falling more in love each day. I know her mind; I know her heart; I know her voice; I know her personality; I know her likes and dislikes: what lines to cross, what lines to not cross, and what lines to avoid like the plague! And best of all, she knows me. It hasn't always been easy, but it's been worth it for the love between us. *And a threefold cord is not quickly broken* (Ecclesiastes 4:12).

Life with Holy Spirit is like a marriage. Holy Spirit was given to us by the Father to teach us all things. (See John 14:26.) Just as with a good teacher, the relationship goes beyond mere instruction and obedience. Holy Spirit is here to mentor us, to lead us—yes, and more so: to cause us to desire and follow the will of God for ourselves. See, I can program a robot to do what I expect—and it will, depending on how good an engineer I am. But to truly do the will of God from our hearts requires the Spirit of God dwelling inside of us. Holy Spirit is here to make us Sons and Daughters of God.

We need to know the person of Holy Spirit. We need to understand His character, His authority and His nature. We need an intimate understanding of how He operates so we can cooperate in our day to day walk with Him. Holy Spirit wants to be a part of everything we do, everything we face, and everything we think. He wants to lead us, guide us, carry us into deeper places of understanding and partner with us in ways we may not fully understand.

The key factor in this relationship is to know His voice.

Sometimes when I'm tired or distracted, my wife complains that I am not really listening to her. During these times, I reply, *"Yes, dear, I heard everything you said."* And I'll repeat her words verbatim. Which of course, is not what she means. She means that I am not engaged with her. My mind and heart are focused elsewhere. I am distracted and not giving her my full attention. It is the same with God. Knowing scripture to quote is not enough. We have to give Him our full attention. We have to engage with Him.

Because we rarely hear Holy Spirit with our natural ears, it is important to spend quality time seeking Him in the realm that He dwells: the spirit. But tuning in to the spiritual realm is not enough. There are many voices in the spiritual world. Our spiritual ears are like radios which can be tuned to different frequencies. We have to learn which one is from Holy Spirit and which are from our minds, our flesh, the enemy, or those of other people, past and present, winds of spiritual power released during their lives and still active today.

The most important thing we will learn in our relationship with Holy Spirit is the discernment of His voice apart from all others. Let's face it: many voices sound like God. And some of the most confused people we know are not those who never tune into the spiritual realm, but those who do so without proper discernment. In the world of the spirit, there is fresh water and salt water. Both will lift us and carry us. But there is only one water which we can drink and live. The fresh water of God brings life. The salt water of the enemy brings confusion, doubt, fear, famine, and ultimately: death. We must learn the difference. Holy Spirit is here to teach us that difference.

Much of what I teach in this book comes from experience. I will share many of my life's adventures in the hope that people can learn from them. More so, I pray that these experiences encourage others to venture forth and develop their own experiences. Stepping out in the voice of God is risky; we will make mistakes. Father God knows this, but there is no other way to learn. A rich man was once asked how he grew so wealthy. He said that he had learned to make right decisions. Well, how did he learn to make right decisions? Experience, he said. And how did he get experience? Making wrong decisions, he said.

We are going to make mistakes, but mistakes are a necessary part of learning. The God who promises in Jeremiah 29:11:

> *For I know the thoughts that I think toward you, says the LORD, thoughts of peace and not of evil, to give you a future and a hope,*

…knows He is dealing with lumpy clay. (My momma named me right!) It is God's job to make us pure. It is our job to submit to the process. And before we can submit to God, we must be able to hear and discern the voice of God.

Discerning the voice of Holy Spirit

The enemy knows we want to grow, and he will do everything in his power to stop us. The weapons at his command include fear, doubt, confusion, and deception. Satan works through our flesh—the areas of our life which God is still reclaiming—and whispers things so clever, we think we thought it up ourselves. The good news is that when we learn to recognize the voice of God, it will silence the words of the enemy and neutralize the feelings of our flesh.

Here is what Jesus said about recognizing the voice of God:

> *And when he <the shepherd> brings out his own sheep,*

he goes before them; and the sheep follow him, for they know his voice. Yet they will by no means follow a stranger, but will flee from him, for they do not know the voice of strangers. (John 10:4-5)

My sheep hear My voice, and I know them, and they follow Me. (John 10:27)

Please note here that Jesus does not say that the sheep won't *hear* the voice of the stranger; he says that they won't *follow* the voice of a stranger because they do not know the stranger's voice. The sheep will follow the voice they know: that of their shepherd.

Essentially, if we have a niggle of doubt, a question, if something does not feel quite right, if the voice we are hearing does not sound like God, if we don't sense the fruit of Holy Spirit manifesting within us as we listen to a voice, there's a good chance it is not God. The differences will become clearer as we clearly hear from God.

At a minimum, we should expect confirmation, both from scripture and from other Christians who know us, before stepping out into something risky. God will take us slowly in learning His voice. God's first words to us will not ask us to sell our house, empty our bank account, or sacrifice a child. When Abraham received the word from God to tie Isaac to the alter, he had a lifetime of hearing the voice of God; there was no doubt as to who he was hearing. As we learn the voice of God in small things, the difference between Him and the enemy will become more apparent, and this is what God wants.

Again, let me say that the least sane people in this life are not those who cannot hear in the spirit, but those who hear without discernment. The miracle of salvation's relationship with God is not that we hear spiritual things. It is that we hear God!

I'm not saying we aren't going to hear the voice of the enemy. In fact, we need to hear the enemy in order to learn the difference. He will speak and try to sow doubt and unbelief. But the voice of God, which we are learning in depth, will neutralize the flesh and silence the enemy's words, causing them to fade harmless from our consciousness like bullets fired into deep water.

The World

All believers hear the voice of God. However, not all believers recognize the voice of God. We are capable of hearing many things, and until we are trained, we can never be sure whether we are hearing last night's pizza, or the novel we read until 2 am, or the voice of our mother's childhood scolding. Our present mental and emotional state also affects our perceptions and causes us to experience things outside of our normal consciousness. When our hearts are broken, for example, we are often receptive to deeper emotional communication. Which is why so many popular books and songs are written around a lost love. The writers know that people experiencing heartbreak are more receptive to heart-level messages.

We need to learn the difference between God's voice and the voices of this present age. While voices in today's world can be evil, not all are evil. Some are simply not appropriate for certain situations. Some influences are aligned with God's will for us; others are not. There is a time to put on weepy songs and mourn a lost love, and there is a time to rise up in power, change into a fresh shirt, and go out to meet the day. There is a time to analyze, plan and strategize, and another time to go forth and conquer. (I believe Ecclesiastes has something to say about that.) Wise discernment knows the difference.

Our Emotions

When we are properly aligned with God, Holy Spirit will begin to penetrate our being and lead us into His will, even when our flesh-driven emotions are saying something different. Now don't get me wrong: nothing is wrong with emotions (feelings) in and of themselves. The trouble is that emotions can be used by either side: good or evil. Because of this, we cannot always trust emotions. We must trust God and allow our emotions to come into alignment with God.

Yes, our emotions can lie to us, especially in the face of a new plan, decision, or endeavor. When we are still in the mode of listening to our flesh, our emotions are not the best indicators of God's will for us. For example: ever feel like not going to work? Skipping church? Ignoring prayer? Hoarding instead of giving? Or in the positive: ever set out on a course of action full of good feelings and brimming confidence, only to run straight into disaster, defeat, and despair? While healthy emotions are to be treasured—they are indeed a gift of God—when emotions and Holy Spirit are in conflict, we must look past our feelings to understand clearly what God is saying to us.

I Corinthians 12:11 says: *But the one and the same spirit works all these things, distributing to each one individually as He wills.* Holy Spirit has a will. When His will and our will align, our feelings follow. We should trust God first, our feelings second.

Our Flesh

As I said before, there are many voices out there. God has a voice, the enemy has a voice, even our parents have a voice echoing within us all our days: *"Clean your room, take out the garbage, tuck in your shirt, stand up straight, get a haircut, don't fight your brother, look out for your sister!"* The body also has a voice—at least mine does. At Thanksgiving it says, *"Eat another piece of cherry pie."* At Christmas, it says, *"Grab the last drumstick."* My body has even been known to quote scripture! I get on a treadmill and pretty soon it is saying, *"Bodily exercise profits little."* Looks like a few of us have heard the same voice!

There is also a voice of our flesh. One telltale sign of this voice is that the flesh always rebels against God. However, the rebellion is usually not a head-on battle, but instead, a subtle, guerilla war. Take tithing, for example. Rather than screaming, *"Tithing is wrong,"* the flesh will rationalize and say, *"Tithing is not for today."* Catch the difference? Most Christians would jump in alarm if they heard that giving to God was wrong. But by relegating tithing to an Old Testament custom, it "frees" them from a present obligation in the guise of grace verses law. If they continue listening to the voice of flesh, they will likely stop giving altogether, and this stops the flow of God's blessing to them.

Sometimes the flesh imitates the voice of God in order to steer us off course. It will excuse us from efforts which we really don't want to do anyway. *"You know, you don't have to do this…"* or *"you don't feel like it today, so why bother?"* For example, the flesh will rarely say: *"Ignore your fellow Christians and separate yourself from fellowship."* That would throw up a red flag. Instead, it will say: *"You need rest. God gave a day of rest. Sleep in today, and tomorrow, and next week. Come to think of it: quit going to that church 30 miles away and start looking for a church 5 miles away."* In the end, the person stops going to church all together, which is what the flesh was aiming for all along.

The marked difference between the voice of flesh and the voice of God is the resultant faith produced. Faith can be positive or negative, leading us towards God or away from God. The things the flesh tells me to do are based on a negative view of God: His power in my life and my own power as His creation. The flesh will tell me I can do things harmful to my body, even though it is a temple of Holy Spirit. It will tell me not to try something new because I risk failure, even though I have the promise of God that I will prosper and mature. It will tell me to stay safe at home and fear the unknown, even though no weapon formed against me will prosper.

The voice of God, on the other hand, is a clarion call to step up, shore up, man-up and woman-up! It results in faith towards God, alignment with the written word of God, and harmony with God's people. It calls us to be better than we might see ourselves at present. It called Gideon out of hiding, it called Moses from the desert, it called Jesus out of the garden of Gethsemane, and it calls us daily to our destiny.

When judging if a voice, a direction, a nudging or instinct is from God or not, we must ask ourselves where our faith is being directed and who or what is being glorified. When God speaks, our faith leaps in His direction. It energizes us, empowers us, and fills us with His grace. It calls us to step out of our boat and into His reality. It is sent to accomplish all that God wants to do, and it will not return to Him void. It cries, *"Get up! Get going! Do all that is in your heart, for I am with you."*

Personal Relationship with Holy Spirit

Holy Spirit wants to be personable with us. He wants to communicate with us so that He can bring us into a place of deep trust and communion. In Ephesians 5:18, we are told: *do not be drunk with wine, but be filled with the Spirit.* Having an intimate relationship with Holy Spirit is vital to our discernment. Jesus said: *My sheep hear my voice...* (John 10:27), but in order to be one of His sheep, we have to follow the Shepherd. Our discernment of His voice is contingent on being a part of Him and His works.

A man I know was on his first backpacking trip with friends in the Cascade mountains. His first night out, as he was bedding down for sleep, he heard from a distance a high-pitched wailing sound, like an animal in distress. Concerned, he woke his friend sleeping beside him—an experienced mountain-man—and asked him what that sound was. *"That's a bear,"* said the sleepy mountain-man. *"It's trying to trick the dogs into coming out of camp so it can eat them."* Then the man grunted *"Stay!"* to his dogs and went back to sleep. See, the bear was afraid to come into the camp. The only way it could attack the dogs was to trick them into coming out from the safety of the man's protection. Fortunately for the dogs that night, they did not fall for the bear's ruse, but followed their master's voice.

Obedience

As we learn to recognize Holy Spirit through discernment and intimate relationship, the next step is to learn obedience to Him. How many of us have ever needed to make a decision and needed Holy Spirit's help? In John 14:26, it says: *"But the Helper, the Holy Spirit, whom the Father will send in My name, He will teach you all things, and bring to your remembrance all things that I said to you.*

In the same verse, the Amplified Bible includes these words to describe Holy Spirit:

> *the Comforter,*
>
> *the Counselor,*

the Helper,

the Intercessor,

the Advocate,

the Stand-By.

At times, I travel over 200,000 miles a year and need to be at the right place at the right time. I can't afford to be at the wrong place at the wrong time. I always pray and check my "Knower." I want to know what is going on from God's perspective. Is this the plane I'm supposed to get on? Am I NOT supposed to get on this plane? I want a word from God regarding that plane. And having received that word, it is up to me to obey it. Having the word is not enough; obeying is what brings the power of God's word into our lives.

In 1996, when Value-Jet flight 592 crashed into the Florida everglades, killing everyone onboard, there was one man who was about to get onboard and suddenly pulled his boarding pass, electing not to fly. The interesting thing is that the man did the same thing on a flight out of Portland, Oregon, 24 years prior, and that flight also crashed. That man knows the word of God when it comes to flying and he obeys it. I want to be like that man! I want to hear from God *before* He says, *"Well done, my good and faithful servant. Enter into your rest."*

A mother told me that one night around 11:00 p.m., she felt the need to get out of bed and pray for her daughter who was out on a date. She obeyed and interceded for about 20 minutes until a peace came to her. At 11:35 p.m., her daughter came home. Her curfew was later, but she came through the door and went straight to her mother's room, saying, *"Were you praying for me?"*

Her mother said, *"Yes."*

The daughter said, *"Mom, I was in a very compromising place, in a moment of weakness. I was ready to give away my purity, but all of a sudden I knew God had revealed it to you and I knew you were interceding for me so I wouldn't make a bad decision."*

Through intimate relationship with Holy Spirit, we can live

in that capacity where we hear God in crises situations and pray through, delivering ourselves or standing in the gap for someone else. It takes both hearing and obeying.

Holy Spirit in the Prophetic Ministry

Luke 12:12 says: *for Holy Spirit will teach you in that very hour what you ought to say.* This scripture is talking about more than personal direction; it is talking about hearing the voice of God as the cornerstone of the prophetic ministry. The prophetic is not about speaking for God; it is about hearing from God. Let me repeat:

> *The prophetic is not about speaking for God; it is about hearing from God.*

In the flow of the apostolic anointing which I am a part of, there is a lot of prophecy spoken. Unfortunately, I have come to learn that some of the people prophesying have not really heard from God. I know this because I've heard prophecies over the years that speak about specific events and times which never came to pass. If we are going to speak for God, we must first learn to truly hear from God. Bob Dylan wrote: *"I'll know my song well before I start singing."* We as ministers of God's word must heed that advice. Open your mouth when you know you have heard something from God. Otherwise, keep it closed.

Holy Spirit as A Leader of Modern Technology

Thousands of years ago, God looked down upon the efforts of evil men and decided that they needed to be frustrated. At the time, they were building a tower to heaven. In reality, it was a monument to the pride of man—a sharp stick aimed at the eye of God. Now, God could have done many things to stop their progress. He could have destroyed the tower. He could have brought famine and misery. He could have given them pro-football, big-screen TVs, and lounge chairs. But He didn't. Instead, He changed their languages—every person's language. In a flash, God struck and nobody could understand anyone else. It didn't take long before they all scattered. They probably reacted the same way we do today when we aren't understood, muttering to themselves: *"These idiots don't get it!"*

Holy Spirit—as facilitator of communication—has been leading man back from that gulf ever since, bridging the gap between people-groups through the redemptive power of Jesus. When Jesus arose, it was Holy Spirit's turn to saddle-up and begin His work on earth. In this redemptive age of man's salvation through Jesus Christ, the creative power to overcome our diversity is bringing together a church long separated by artificial barriers. At the church I presently pastor, we stream our services over the Internet to other churches and actually take questions from people hundreds of miles away. This is the realization of the fundamental aspect of the church: We are ONE!

Holy Spirit wants to lead Christians in all areas of life. India—a country of 350 million gods—is a leader in technical creativity which is bringing the world together. The same technology is being used by the church to advance communications throughout the world. Certainly, some of the technological developments are coming from Christians—India is a diverse country—but most of it is coming from people who are not born-again, people who have no professed relationship with Jesus Christ, who have no understanding of Holy Spirit, and yet are world leaders in technologies being used by God to further His kingdom.

Imagine the uses of advanced virtual conferencing where people thousands of miles apart are so life-like, it is as if they are in the same room! Think of doing a concert in Sydney, Australia, and streaming it live all over the world. Imagine this technology in colleges: an instructor in Phoenix teaching students in Tennessee. And this creativity is coming out of a people who serve 350 million gods! How can this be? It is pure creativity, unity as God intended, and it is being used to bring good things to the earth.

Now, if this is what the unsaved are doing, what potential lies with the children of God?

Holy Spirit as Guide

Years ago, while pioneering a church in the Midwest United States, I was driving down a country road in Missouri and Holy

Spirit said, *"Turn in there!"*

I knew it was the voice of God and yet I drove on. Then I began to wonder, *"Was that God? Or was that me?"* I felt convicted so I gave up struggling, turned around, and drove back to where I was when He spoke. I found myself in front of a house and Holy Spirit said, *"Turn in there."*

As I walked to the house, a bewildered-looking woman stepped outside, walked towards me and said, *"You're the preacher, aren't you?"* Right then, I knew God was up to something. At the time, I was bi-vocational, managing a fuel oil company as well as pastoring a church. I had a 55-gallon drum of cotton spindle oil on the back of my truck which I'd picked up in Sikeston, Missouri. There was nothing about me that said "preacher." (I hadn't even taken an offering yet!) But I knew that God was in this, so I simply said, *"Yes ma'am, I am."* She said, *"My brother-in-law is inside; he's very sick. My sister—his wife—just died and he hasn't eaten in several days. I'm afraid for his life."*

When I walked into the house, sitting in a putrid, broken-down easy chair was the fattest man I'd ever seen. I found out later that he weighed 700 pounds and had actually been on the television show: <u>That's Incredible</u>. I thought: *He's stopped eating? Good for him!* But I knew it wasn't good. He was going to die if he didn't get help. He could not move. The house reeked. And like his easy chair, he was broken. As we began to talk, I sensed his heart and was able to lead him to the Lord. Remarkably, he responded immediately to the Spirit of God and began to pray in a heavenly prayer language. It was glorious to see God touch him. Unfortunately, I knew I'd never be able to baptize him—it was physically impossible until he dropped a few hundred pounds, which he eventually did! My wife and I saw him several months later. He had started a healthy diet, was holding down a good job, and had already dropped to a svelte 500 pounds! Compared to the man I had first met, he was looking great. God's change of that man was all over his face. I was glad I heard Holy Spirit that day and turned around.

Now, I obeyed…that time. But it wasn't always like that. Remember, I said that we learn from our mistakes. We need to heed the lesson. We pass up many more *"turn in there"* commands than we realize, in large part because we are too busy, or too inexperienced, or too scared. So what do we do? Ignore God? No, that is too blatant. Most times we convince ourselves that it wasn't God speaking. *What's God doing, telling me to turn in here, go up to this door, speak to this person? That's invading their privacy. They won't receive me. I could get shot. I'm no good to anyone dead. This can't be God. I gotta pray more. I'm starting to hear voices!*

So we talk ourselves out of it and turn our car radio up a little louder. The sad thing is that people need us; they need the God in us. They need a word of encouragement, a prayer, a demonstration of God's power. Some people are on the verge of giving up. Some are struggling to pay their bills. They're losing homes and jobs and families. To have someone come along and minister as God leads is literally a godsend. God has a people in this world. You picked up this book, so you might be one. The reason God had me write this book was to teach as many as possible to follow God, wherever He might lead.

Romans 8:14 says:

> *For as many as are led by the Spirit of God, they are the sons of God.*

John 16:13 says:

> *However, when He, the Spirit of truth, has come, He will guide you into all truth; for He will not speak on His own authority, but whatever He hears He will speak; and He will tell you things to come.*

God's desire is for every child of His to know how to rely on His Faithful Guide: Holy Spirit. Isaiah 58:11 says:

> *The LORD will guide you continually, and satisfy your soul in drought, and strengthen your bones.....*

Think of a neighbor; does he or she need strengthened? Truth be told, we all need to be stronger. There are unrighteous burdens to be lifted and righteous burdens to be shouldered. Sometimes we need to make tough choices, like casting out a 35 year-old deadbeat son but helping an unwed mother finish her education. God is looking for a people who will do things willingly and wisely. Isaiah 58:11 goes on to say:

> You shall be like a watered garden and like a spring of water whose waters do not fail.

When we flow with Him, our waters will not fail.

Would You Buy a Used Car From Holy Spirit?

My father-in-law was a great man. He and my mother-in-law prayed me into the Kingdom. I appreciate so much all the prayers for me when I was a heathen, running from God.

My father-in-law retired and, along with my mother-in-law, decided to start a used car lot. Now, my father-in-law was not mechanical. Being as gracious as I know how to be: he did not know how to change a spark plug in a lawn mower. When my wife, Susan, told me that her parents were going into the used car business, I thought, *Oh, my goodness!* I was scared they were going to lose all their money. How could he pick a good used vehicle with his lack of mechanical aptitude? Oh me of little faith!

Every time my father-in-law attended the used car auctions in Little Rock, AR, his wife (Susan's mother) would come along and sit off to the side of the bidding, quietly praying in tongues. As each car was brought to the auction floor and examined by the bidders, she'd nod "Yes" or "No" to my father-in-law and he would purchase accordingly. What a system they had! Of the many hundreds of cars they sold over the years, they only had two or three lemons, and these were purchased when my father-in-law went alone.

My own faith grew as I watched God prosper them in a tremendous way. Interestingly, the reason they went back into business in the first place was so they could give to ministries. They already had everything they needed to live on; everything was paid for. They just wanted to give more, and for many years in a little town in Arkansas, they had a business which prospered. Why? Because God gave them a plan which they accepted. He led them into it and they followed, operating together with wisdom.

The "Gifts" of Holy Spirit

I Corinthians 12, is the famous chapter on the gifts of Holy Spirit.

> *Now, concerning spiritual gifts, brethren, I do not want you to be ignorant....*

However, in most Bible translations, that word *"gifts"* is italicized. In Strong's Concordance, that word has 9999 to the side of it. In the study of Greek or Hebrew, an assigned number 9999 means that it does not exist. In all five of the original manuscripts for this letter of Paul's, the word "gifts" is not there. In I Corinthians 14:1, the other famous chapter about gifts, it is not there either. It was inserted by translators; it does not exist in the original manuscripts. In truth, there are NOT nine gifts of the Spirit as listed in I Corinthians 12. There is one gift: Holy Spirit. The confusion comes from the fact that there are nine *manifestations* of that gift.

For years, I taught this subject in error until Holy Spirit corrected me. I was intent on discovering a person's spiritual gift, and I probably drove hundreds into nervous breakdowns trying to help them find it. My breakthrough finally came—thanks to the prayers of those I'd nearly driven crazy—when I stopped teaching on discovering the personal gifts of Holy Spirit and began to teach people how to fall in love with the gift of Holy Spirit. Suddenly, they were prophesying, laying hands on the sick, speaking in tongues, receiving words of knowledge and wisdom, moving in miracles and healing. When they began to move in all nine manifestations, their lives were changed. It was all out of relationship with Holy Spirit. The gift *IS* Holy Spirit. When He comes into our lives, He begins to unwrap Himself "nine ways to Sunday."

Imagine giving a person a Harley Davidson motorcycle. The gift is the motorcycle, but the manifestation of the gift is what they do with it: delivering newspapers, taking road trips, carrying the homeless to church (one at a time, of course). These are the manifestations of the gift; they are not the gift. And the more the person rides the Harley, the better they come to understand the bike: its handling, performance, and the funny noises it makes, which on a Harley, usually means it needs more gas, oil, or chrome.

When we have communion through a personal relationship with Holy Spirit, we begin to understand His full personality and its manifestations, not just a narrow aspect of Him. We need to cast aside our preconceived notions of who Holy Spirit is and how He operates in order to fully receive Him. This requires a special silence, as David said in Psalms. 131:2,

Surely I have calmed and quieted my soul,

Like a weaned child with his mother;

Like a weaned child is my soul within me.

This works in human relationships as well. We can be with a loved-one for hours, never uttering a word, and in the end we will know each other better than when we started. Which is good, because on a Harley, it's too noisy to talk anyway.

Nudgings...Personable

As we understand the personality of Holy Spirit, we begin to understand the nudging of Holy Spirit. What do I mean by "nudging?" Glad you asked! At the time of this writing, my wife and I will soon celebrate our 37th wedding anniversary. And yet after these many years, I can call home from the ends of the earth and ask her how things are going, and I know before she answers me, how things really are. She tries to protect me from worry by saying, *"Oh, everything's fine,"* but I know it's not. So I'll say, *"What's wrong?"* And after a little prodding, she'll come out with it. See, I can hear it in her voice; I can sense that something's wrong with the church, our children, or her. I just know it—anything less than complete honesty between us is pointless.

When I'm at home, I can walk in the house and feel something unusual. She might be busy with a chore in another room, but I'll feel it in the air. Something's not right. Or something is very right! It

What

is?

works in the positive too. There is often a spirit of celebration in our house. Or a deep, abiding peace. In fact, that is generally how things are with us, now that we've learned a thing or two about how to get along in the Lord. Since my house is so blessed, it is the negatives which stand out as unusual.

My wife and I have become one. We are not just intimate; we are friends who communicate on a fundamental level that only deep trust can convey: a trust built up over years.

Life with Holy Spirit can have the same level of communication. There are mornings when He wakes me up with a song, an idea, or a blessing. It's like He's glad to see me. (He's never told me to brush my teeth, but I'm sure that day is coming.) Throughout the day, I'll get a sense, an inclination, a sudden idea that something ought to be done, and when I act on it, I see the larger plan of God unfold. But it takes my initial faith to act when God's inclination towards me is conveyed only through a nudge. It requires <u>sensitivity.</u>

Now, I did not just step into this level of relationship. It took years of practice. In the beginning of developing this sensitivity, many people act in the belief that they are hearing God, and sometimes the results are not what God intended. (Most likely because God wasn't in it in the first place.) Learning to detect the nudging of Holy Spirit requires time, experience, and maturity.

Maturity in God does not mean a grave, reserved nature. It means wisdom, experience, skill, cunning, and sometimes requires reckless abandon. It means we know what we are doing. As we mature, it only takes a nudge for Holy Spirit to change our direction, change our day, or change our life. God doesn't want to waste time and energy dropping an atomic bomb on our head to get our attention. He'd much rather tap our shoulder, whisper in our ear, and be heard for who He is: GOD! Remember Elisha on the mountain? God wasn't in the earthquake; He wasn't in the whirlwind; He was in the still, small voice. It takes sensitivity to hear God like that. And that comes with quality time together. *He that has ears to hear….*

Intercession

There are times when Holy Spirit simply prays through us. Romans 8:27 says:

Now He who searches the hearts knows what the mind of the Spirit is, because He makes intercession for the saints according to the will of God.

Indeed, this is how I came to be baptized in the Holy Spirit. After I was born again, my wife and I lived in the same little town in Arkansas. We attended two churches there. One was a United Methodist church where our families were formal members. The other was a Baptist Church where we attended Bible study with a great friend of ours, Tommy Lalman.

One night, Tommy had a severe asthma attack and had to be rushed to the hospital. He was at death's door and I prayed everything I knew to pray that night. But somehow I knew that I hadn't touched God like I needed to. So I told Susan: *"I want you to send the kids over to your mother's. We are going to have a Bible Study and a prayer meeting here. Just you and I."*

We knelt and began talking to God, something like: *"God, there has to be more of You than what we've got. We want what You've got. And heal Tommy!"* And that's when we began to speak in tongues. A strange language poured out of us and the power of God manifested in the flow. But because there was no church in our town that would accept tongues, we had never heard them before. Still, we knew it was good, and the witness of Holy Spirit was too great to hold back.

Tommy recovered, but Susan and I never have. Praise God! But just as I knew that God had done a work in us that night, I also knew that this in-filling of Holy Spirit would cost us. We were asked to leave the United Methodist church. So we formally joined the Baptist church—the only other church in town—and eventually we were asked to leave there too! To this day, I have nothing against the Methodists or the Baptists. Ours was simply a traditional town which worshipped God traditionally. Actually, things worked out wonderfully because the rejections caused us to plant our first church. Since that time, God has led us across the South, planting churches. We are now on our 18th church and will continue as long as we are led.

Sealed by Holy Spirit

In Ephesians 4:30, it says:

And do not grieve the Holy Spirit of God, by whom you were sealed for the day of redemption.

What does it mean to be "sealed?" It means that we have been given a down payment on our redemption. Think of it as earnest money or a promissory note. It essentially means that God is not done with us yet, but He promises to complete the work He has started. It means: hold on, stand fast, and see the salvation of our Lord come to pass.

God has sealed us by Holy Spirit. He has covered us by Jesus' blood. We have His word to guide us and shield us. But understand that we don't just live by the written word today. We live by every word that *proceeds* from the mouth of God—not just every word that *has proceeded*. When Paul wrote to the Ephesians, God was actively speaking. That is where the New Testament came from. And yet, God is still speaking today. Why? Well, because He still has things to say. Imagine that! The God of creation still wishes to speak to His creatures. What a thought!

Certainly, God speaks through the written word. But He goes beyond that, just as a man might speak and teach beyond the particular books he's written. Certainly, anything spoken by God will line up with His Bible; that is what it's for. But so much more needs to be covered. For example, my friend David Reeves received a word once that he was to move to Oxford, Mississippi, and start a church there. Now, he could have searched the Bible all day long, but he would never have found the word "Oxford" anywhere on those sacred pages. Nowhere does it say, *"Move your family to Oxford."* I guess if he'd been called to Nineveh, he'd have been OK. But Oxford? No such luck. Now, God does say in Isaiah that we will *"go out with joy, and be led forth with peace."* And when David considered the move to Oxford, he felt peace and joy towards God, in confirmation of that word. But David had to be able to hear God for himself regarding the move to Mississippi.

God speaks in alignment with His written word, and yet He speaks beyond that sacred text. He has spoken great things and He will speak even greater things in the days to come. Amen!

Holy Spirit as General Overseer

Therefore take heed to yourself and to all the flock among which the Holy Spirit has made you overseers, to the Shepherd for the church of God which He has purchased with his own blood. (Acts 20:28)

Few people think of Holy Spirit as an overseer of the churches, yet that is exactly what it says in scripture. In essence, it means that we have to follow Holy Spirit. He desires to lead the churches through His voice. In Revelation 2:29, it says: *He who has an ear, let him hear what the Spirit says to the churches.* Holy Spirit expects to be followed. While Holy Spirit is seeking to speak to us, we should be seeking Holy Spirit's leadership. We need His input and His wisdom. We need to be aligned with His purposes. The scripture that we all know is this: *where the spirit of the Lord is, there is liberty* (II Corinthians 3:17). However, the original text says it greater: *Where the Spirit IS LORD, there is liberty.* Holy Spirit is in many churches, but He isn't *Lord* in many churches.

It is quite possible to continue a ministry without submitting to Holy Spirit's lordship. People do it all the time. However, this cannot continue for long before the very life of God is lost. The deception is that the form will continue long after the life has bled from it. The church building will continue to stand, people will continue arriving for service, the choir will sing the same spirited songs, the offerings will be full, but something will be missing. Those most sensitive to God will be the first to raise concern and eventually leave, but they will be replaced by others who are less sensitive, people who like what they see: a shiny building, clean choir robes, green plants in the vestibule and plenty of paved parking. The emphasis will shift from hearing God to doing those things which increase attendance. In the end—and there will be an end—the works of God will be replaced by the works of man. On the surface, things will appear to be growing and thriving. Only after the cataclysmic collapse will folks ring the smoldering ruins, stare into the crater and cry: *"What happened?"*

If we expect Holy Spirit to assume a position of Overseer, a reverence and a fear of God needs to return to our lives and our churches. I believe God wants to invade us with holiness but it must be true Biblical holiness. It won't be about the way we look on the outside; it's going to be about the way we conduct ourselves on the inside. The outside will follow the inside. Holiness is a reverence for God—an awe of God. In some ways, we have become so familiar with God that we cheapen Him and "brother" Him down to our level. He wasn't created in our image. We were created in His image. When we grasp this revelation, Holy Spirit will enter the church in greater measure than we have ever imagined!

As overseer of the church, Holy Spirit will bring alignment between God's people and their life-callings. Christians need to understand that God calls everyone, yet not all callings are to full-time ministry. Businesspeople need not leave their occupations in order to serve God. Mothers and housewives need not leave their families in order to be true to God. Yes, there are secular callings as much as there are five-fold ministry callings of God.

People need to understand their true calling. Because of the prestige associated with full-time ministry, Christians tend to gravitate towards that area of service. However, some people are truly called to the marketplace. Some are also called to ministry-shared vocations. Some are called exclusively to ministry. Paul did both— work and minister. Joseph, once he got out of prison, was primarily a government official. David was a king as well as a minister. Daniel was strictly a prophet and a mystic. Evangelists make great salespeople. Prophets can lead companies. And some apostles should run for government offices. Let us be released to serve God in our true callings.

I serve God because of the call on my life; I truly believe I am doing what God has called me to do. When God first called me, I turned my back and ran. When I finally stopped running and became born again, I was a full-time businessman. My father and I owned many corporations together. Later, I received a revelation about being unequally yoked with unbelievers, so I paid a lawyer to divide all those businesses so that I would not be unequally yoked to my unbelieving father. Of course, it hurt my father deeply—broke his heart. But in the long run, it also got him saved. He didn't understand what I was doing at the time, and I didn't understand it fully either—I just obeyed. But God worked through it and brought my Dad's heart to Him. My Dad lived well into his eighties, loving God and loving life. He was my best friend. This was all possible because I was faithful to my true calling and God was faithful to both of us.

Holy Spirit Responsibilities

Holy Spirit has been given two special responsibilities.

His first responsibility is to take the place of Jesus on the earth. Since the resurrection, Jesus is our Advocate in heaven. He sits at the right hand of the Father, making intercession for us. Putting it in layman's terms, He is saying: *"Father, give Holy Spirit a nudge so He can help Clay. Go to those people he's working with. Fall upon them in power so that their eyes see and their ears hear. Help him to reach the people tonight, better than he's ever done before."*

As intercessor, Jesus is making a better case for me than the greatest lawyer in a courtroom. He's my best advocate; He's my best lawyer. He's pleading my case right now, causing the Father to send Holy Spirit in accordance with my needs and His will. *"Father, give him another nudge. OK—he didn't get it. Give him a BIGGER nudge. Better yet, whack him! OK, there you go. He's looking up. All right, now give him some supernatural endowment and let's get him out there to teach, farther than he's ever gone before."*

I don't care how I get it, as long as I get it. Amen.

The second responsibility of Holy Spirit is to show Jesus to the world. When we see actions and manifestations of Holy Spirit, we are seeing Jesus—the real Jesus. We need to know Jesus as He really is, not as church tradition has taught us. The traditions of men make the Word of God of no effect. I seek the Jesus who is revealed through Holy Spirit: the Jesus who can heal, preach, teach, love, prophesy, open blind eyes, set captives free. And if He turns my water bottle into wine, so be it, just not while I'm driving!

The fact that we experience Jesus supernaturally through Holy Spirit does not necessarily make us super Christians. At times in my ministry, I have struggled with doubt and unbelief, and yet God performed miracles in spite of me. I've seen cancer tumors drop off of Navaho women, falling to the ground and melting like dry ice. I've seen blind eyes opened. I've seen the tongue of a spiritual son, who was being very disrespectful at the time, cleave to the roof of his mouth so he could not talk until he repented! I've seen almost every miracle imaginable. It is Holy Spirit who does those things and He does them for one reason: to show Jesus on the earth. We need this in our nation. We need this in our world. We need signs that will shake religion and end the strife between Liberals and Conservatives, Believers and Atheists, Baptists and Pentecostals, Republicans and Environmentalists, *Bikers who stare at Cowboys who are laughing at the Hippies who are praying they'll get out of here alive!* (David Alan Coe) I'm praying He sends so much new wine that it bursts our old wineskins, drenches everybody, and gets us all out of here alive!

I believe our God is able to do what He says He will do. I further believe that as we hear the voice of God and act on it, we will see things greater than we ever have before. I believe we will see miracles not dreamed of in these times. God is going to do what He has proclaimed. A friend of mine (Harold Eberle) wrote a series on the spirituality of Christianity. He started out by saying: *Remove the supernatural from Christianity, and you no longer have Christianity.* We need to get a hold of that revelation through communion with Holy Spirit, understanding His will and moving in His power.

Chapter 2
The Blessing of Hearing Holy Spirit

In Chapter 1, we discussed recognizing the voice of God through Holy Spirit. In this chapter, I want to expand on the blessings of hearing Holy Spirit. In Hebrews 3:7-8, the author brings out an important aspect to this:

> *Therefore, as the Holy Spirit says: "Today, if you will hear His voice, do not harden your hearts as in the rebellion,"*

Notice the determinant in the verse: *Today if you WILL hear...*

Hearing Holy Spirit is an act of our will. As such, we decide whether to hear or not hear. Now, this may seem strange to those who try to hear Holy Spirit and simply conclude that they are spiritually deaf. But this scripture says that hearing God is a function of our will.

Anything that involves our will also involves our authority. *"I will"* is a powerful declaration. So powerful, in fact, that the enemy does not want it revealed just how powerful we are when we speak it, so he disguises the fact that we even have such power, all the while using our will against us.

We find evidence of this when we look behind our actions to the core decisions governing our lives. If we look further into those decisions, we will find *"I will"* statements. They can be overtly positive, negative, or somewhere in between.

I will arise every morning and pray.

I will seek God with my whole heart.

I will love my neighbor as myself.

I will make my child learn piano.

I will never let a person hurt me again.

I will have more fun in life than these Christians I know.

Behind each *"I will"* statement is our personal authority leading to the actions which fill our lives.

Yes, all human beings have authority. We decide many things affecting our lives. However, Christian believers have greater authority, as our authority assimilates the power of God whenever we surrender to His authority.

Authority is transferred through surrender. I can choose to operate on my personal authority for certain decisions or I can surrender my authority to a greater power. For example, if I tried to stop a robbery in progress, I might be successful on my own, provided the robbers listened to me. However, if I wanted greater authority, I could dial 911 and wait for the police to show up. On my own, I could say to the robbers: *"Stop in the name of the law."* (Catchy phrase, eh?) And the robbers would laugh me silly. But with a brief phone call, six police cars arrive, an armed SWAT team would descend from the ceiling, and the laughing would be over. That is the power of authority transfer. That is the power our God extends to us through surrender of our authority to His authority.

In applying this principle, I wake up everyday saying, *"Lord I give you total authority in my life today."* I've seen the results of this position before God, and they are powerful. I've spoken words to people which they desperately needed to hear. I've taken authority over things which would have destroyed me on my own. I've seen bigger things move than I ever dreamed could be moved at my command alone.

Let me be clear: my Father and I have greater authority than I do on my own. And by rising up every morning and saying *"Father, I give you authority in my life today,"* He rebukes the enemies from my life. We win battles when I don't fight alone. My fight is His fight, my enemies are His enemies, my strength is His strength, and my life...well, you can figure that one out.

On a trip to Amsterdam, a young woman demonically manifested before my eyes, and yet God delivered her by His authority. I was ministering in church and a group of gang members came in to service. I taught for a while and then gave an alter call for salvation. Three of the gang members came forth. They gave their hearts to God and one even took off his colors and stomped it. It was great victory for the Lord. To stomp your gang colors is the ultimate dishonor towards the gang. It can lead to death.

As Holy Spirit ministered to these new converts, a girl who had come with them (but who was not dressed in gang attire) fell on the floor and began writhing like snake, even flashing her tongue in and out. She came slithering to the front of the church. It was obviously demonic and deeply frightening. The leadership of the church fled the building, leaving me behind. The gang members—not knowing enough to be fearful—asked how they could help. Through the power of Holy Spirit, we all prayed and she was delivered, then saved, by the power of God through the blood of Jesus. Glory to God!

We make a decision to hear the voice of God. We can tune our ear to Him or tune it to other things. The problem is that we've tuned ourselves in other directions for so long, we don't realize there are other settings on our dial. Finding God's "station" takes time and practice but it can be done. Indeed, this is how it is done: *"I will hear...."*

How many of us have children and find that to really hear what they are saying, we need to reorient our hearts in their direction? When my three year-old granddaughter starts talking to me, I have to bend down low to hear her. I also have to stop my mind from spinning in the direction it was going and redirect it in her direction. To do this, it helps to remind myself of the things which might be important to a three year-old. I turn my heart to her heart in order to find out. I tune my ear to her voice. I idle my own internal engine. Once I have done all these things, I take a deep breath...and wait. Sometimes, she comes right out with whatever is on her mind. Other times, it takes a few tries but she eventually gets it. And if I've stayed tuned to her as she works through it, I get it too.

Now, God is not a three-year old, but the principle is the same. We turn our heart to God, we tune our ear to God, we stop our internal churning, we wait...and listen...and hear.

People in Authority—Recognizing Holy Spirit On Our Own

Immediately after the terrorist attacks on September 11th, 2001, God said something which shook me up. He said: *"Recognizing the voice of God is no longer optional."* I knew right then that I had to get this message out to the rest of the body. Little did I know at the time how difficult it would be.

In Exodus 20:18-19, we read:

> *Now all the people witnessed the thunderings, the lightning flashes, the sound of the trumpet, and the mountain smoking; and when the people saw it, they trembled and stood afar off. Then they said to Moses, "You speak with us, and we will hear; but let not God speak with us, lest we die."*

Once I read this scripture, I began to understand the difficulty in teaching others to hear the voice of God. These scriptures reveal a dichotomy: Moses preparing to speak to God, and the people trembling, backing up, deathly afraid to even hear God. This is the Old Testament model for interactions between God and Man. Priests and Prophets communicate with God and pass the word on to the common people. However, this is not the New Testament model. Today, we understand ourselves to be *a chosen generation, a **royal priesthood**, a holy nation, His own special people…"* (I Peter 2:9).

But does everybody believe this?

Despite what they may profess, many of the men and women of God who lead churches don't want the people of God to become empowered to recognize the voice of God on their own. I know this because I see their actions, and their actions contradict their professed goals. The government structure we have in many churches encourages leaders to hoard power in order to survive. In these congregations, it is difficult for people of God to step into positions of spiritual leadership without threatening those at the top who control the organizational power.

Now, I'm not saying everybody with a quiver in their liver should take the pulpit on any given Sunday. But I am saying that as long as we view a person with a proven ability to hear God as something extraordinary— above the "common people"—we will tend to elevate these individuals to positions they were not meant to occupy, empowering them to climb the mountain for us as we shrink back in fear or laziness. Later, we will cry foul when they fail to live up to our expectations and leave us without the voice of God.

God wants to close the breach between clergy and laity that has been carved by unenlightened people. The Old Testament has been fulfilled. We need to walk in the relationship God has given to ALL BELIEVERS through Jesus.

I serve as a coach in my church. I am there to help the people as much as I am there to lead them. While I do exercise authority, I am not there to raise up a bunch of followers of Clay Nash. Instead, I am there to set the people on the path to the mountain of the living God. I do not do the work for them any more than a basketball coach jumps onto the court and starts shooting three-pointers. The Lord says that it's time for the leaders to get off the court and allow the people of God to arise to His work.

I am pleased to say that there are people in my churches who are more anointed for healing than I am. There are people who have stronger words of knowledge and wisdom than I do. I dare say, some are even much better preachers. I think the only difference between me and them is that I have a louder voice! (That comes from riding a Harley and shouting back to my wife.)

Now, I do hear from God in a unique way. Through Holy Spirit, I've received people's Social Security numbers and relayed them to the individuals. Why? To prove I could steal their identity? No. As a witness to God's supernatural power. God has given me telephone numbers and people's names as well. Again, it's a sign from God to reach those who are in need of Him. Of course, in this age of the internet, those signs might not be as powerful anymore, but God has His ways of moving in every age. I knew of a prophet who told a waitress—a complete stranger—that her son, whom she had not seen in several years, was going to call her at 1:30 p.m. a week from that day. You know what? The son called and they were reconciled. God wants to touch people and He'll do just about anything to reach them.

A leader must raise up people who can hear God in a greater capacity than he or she can. While this might be a threat to some leaders who are intent on preserving control, the leader who truly leads people to God will have no trouble seeing them advance further. Isn't this the progression of the church we all profess to desire? The people we lead should advance beyond us because they stand on our shoulders. They are our glory just as we are the glory of those who came before us. The great cloud of witnesses described in Hebrews celebrates when we accomplish what they could only see by faith during their lifetime.

One of the things the great men and women of faith envisioned in their lifetimes was the growth of the kingdom of God over the whole earth. Unfortunately, things don't appear to be going in that direction. Many people today ignore the church. In the United Kingdom, less than 3% of the nation attends church. But before we beat our breast in horror, let's look at what they are walking away from: a church of spectators watching a few people in front speak for God.

People are changing. The same church structure which reached them 50 years ago is not going to hold them today. The church has to change. What we did during the last decade is not working now. We have preached the Word until it runs out people's ears, down their backs and forms a puddle of Greek letters at their shoes. We have amplified music blaring from our stages in the name of holy celebration, and nobody can hear the person next to them, let alone Holy Spirit. People have been released and admonished and revived and converted so often—sometimes all in one night—that they develop anti-bodies to every Godly appeal. In the end, congregations grow more dependent upon their leaders, waiting for the chosen few to descend the fiery mountain and speak for God.

How about we remove all preaching from our services? If it's not helping, get rid of it! If the music is drowning out our voices, unplug it. Our fellowship needs to be about Holy Spirit. It needs to be about people coming together in Holy Spirit, encountering and reaching and loving one other, ministering to each as the Spirit leads. It is hard to experience our fellow brother or sister when all eyes are riveted to the front and all ears are filled by the voices of the few, the special, the "anointed ones."

We have to get real. Look at the average church. How many people do we find under the age of 25? Not many. Know why? I'll tell you what they tell me: *"Church sucks!"* Now I know that is not a traditionally accepted form of speech, but that is how they communicate as they turn away from our doors. Young people can sense when things are not real, and in this age of instant information, they will turn off the church in a heartbeat if we can't offer them something tangible. Jesus preached far less and did much more than we attempt today.

We have become the fortified church, protecting our safe haven, our comfort zone, our status-quo. Just to get into a church anymore, we have to know the special handshake. We preach against street gangs, but we've become a gang ourselves, requiring our own initiation. If someone approaches a Pentecostal church, they have to bow and cry out in tongues—total surrender. If they approach a Charismatic church, they have to hold their hands high because God is expected to pour out a blessing. If they approach a Catholic church, they have to learn when to kneel and when to genuflect. And don't dare speak out of turn! It seems we have more ways to disqualify folks than to qualify them.

But the good news is that the change has already begun. You can't show me a dying church without finding an emerging church— a true church—rising from the ashes. What is dying is not the church Jesus spoke of but that which man created. The church Jesus gave His life for is the church in which everyone groans to hear from God for themselves. No longer can we resort to: *"Come on apostle, come on pastor, somebody hear God for me."* We all must hear from God. God is speaking today.

Recognizing the voice of God is no longer optional.

Church in Wal-Mart

I was traveling through Tennessee late one afternoon, going to preach in a small church that evening. In those days I used a cordless mic, so I carried my own with me in case the church didn't have one. (Put me on a cord and I don't do real well. Feels too much like a tether.)

That day, I had a spiritual son with me and we stopped at a Wal-Mart to get a 9-volt battery for my microphone. I said, *"I'll get batteries and let's get back in the truck. We're running real tight on time."* Well, never go into Wal-mart looking for batteries when you are tight on time; you will be there a while. I walked down an aisle looking for these elusive batteries, when I passed a young woman and Holy Spirit said, *"Tell her I love her very much and that she's not pregnant, but that she needs to quit fornicating."*

Now, I don't know what kind of relationship most people have with God, but I am pretty open with Him. So I said, *"God, You tell her. She can't slap you."*

He said, *"I'm trying to tell her!"*

So I went back to the young man traveling with me and said, *"I want you to come and stick with me, no matter what happens."*

He gave me a worried look and said, *"You're fixin' to be a prophet in Wal-Mart, aren't you? We're going to get in trouble. I think I'll stay here."*

I said, *"Well, we'll get in trouble together. And we'll get out of trouble together. Come on. You're coming with me."*

So we found the young woman. I eased up beside her and said, *"I know you'll think I'm crazy, but I'm a minister and I feel God said something to me for you."*

Suddenly, I had her attention, so I continued: *"The Lord said to tell you He loves you very much and you're not pregnant but you need to quit fornicating."*

She immediately dropped her head and began to cry. I reached out and laid my hand on her shoulder, asking if I could pray for her. Through her tears, she muttered *"Yes."* As I prayed, she suddenly fell to the floor under the power of God—right there in Wal-Mart! We had a blue light special on aisle number seven! People began to gather around. She finally got up, filled with God, and said, *"I've never fainted like that before."*

She went home that day, kicked her boyfriend out and found a good church. For a few years afterwards, I would get a card from her once a year thanking me. The last time I heard from her, she was teaching a Sunday School class and working with young people.

How many people are we passing by at Wal-Mart? The Lord may want us to speak that kind of word. But first we have to hear that kind of a word, and to do that, we must learn to recognize His voice. Hearing God's voice is not about what it can do for us, but what it can do for others.

Three Promises

There are promises to those who recognize the voice of God. In John 10:27-28, we read:

> *My sheep hear My voice, and I know them, and they follow Me. And I give them eternal life, and they shall never perish; neither shall anyone snatch them out of My hand.*

I read three promises here:

1) We have eternal life,

2) We will never perish,

3) We are secure in Jesus' hand.

Let's take each one individually and see what God is saying to us.

1ˢᵗ Promise: Eternal Life

From these verses, I conclude that eternal life begins with hearing the voice of God. Of course, many of us were taught that eternal life starts when we are "born again." I'm not arguing that being "born again" and eternal life are not related, but let's understand when eternal life starts. It starts with hearing the voice of God.

There is a religious idea in the church which says we receive eternal life after we die. If that is the case, then heaven is full of dead people. Somehow, I don't think that is the case.

2nd Promise: We Will Never Perish

The second promise to those who recognize the voice of God is that they will never perish. This may seem obvious until we realize how many Christians are actually perishing.

There is no greater evidence of Christians perishing than in the family. The divorce rate among born-again, church-going Christians is the same as among non-believing people. As an apostle, I know how many dysfunctional families we have attending our churches. And that's fine if they are being helped; they should be there! I thank God that they are coming. But it's the families who are putting on an image every Sunday which concern me—husbands and wives who can't stand each other, but act like everything's OK, threatening their kids with mortal punishment if they speak out of line, and greeting everybody with a fresh-scrubbed, plastic smile that came straight from their sugar-fortified cereal.

This kind of charade rarely works for long, and it has a greater impact on our ability to recognize the voice of God than we might realize. We tune out the voice of God when we don't want to hear His word on a particular subject. Trouble is, we can't selectively tune God out. If we turn our heart from God on a particular subject, we won't hear anything He is saying to us on any subject. If He is saying,

Work on your marriage.

Get real with your spouse.

Spend time with your kids,

...and we don't want to hear anything on that subject, guess what? We won't hear Him when the car is about to breakdown. We won't hear Him when we hire the accountant who eventually embezzles our money. We won't hear God pleading with us to reach out to our son or daughter before they run away from home. We won't hear any of it because we stopped being open and honest with God in our un-surrendered areas of life—those areas with a self-protecting wall around them.

The results of failing to hear God can be severe. Christians have died prematurely for sad and senseless reasons. One of them—in my opinion—was Keith Green, the Christian singer-songwriter from the 1970's and 80's who died tragically when a plane he owned crashed after take-off. Keith wrote some of the greatest Christian songs we will ever hear. He had a tremendous Psalmist anointing.

So why do I think Keith Green may have missed hearing God at the time of his death? According to the National Transportation Safety Board, he climbed into his ministry's Cessna 414 which was already overloaded with five extra passengers. The pilot also showed a lack of skill and wisdom in allowing this to be done on a hot, humid East-Texas July day when flight required even more engine power. That plane never should have left the ground under those conditions. As it was, it did not get far before they all perished.

Another singer-songwriter whose premature death breaks my heart is Rich Mullins. He was driving a jeep to a benefit concert when he lost control and the jeep flipped over. He and his passenger were not wearing seat belts and were thrown from the car. Rich was injured, laying on the road, and could not move out of the way of an oncoming tractor-trailer which hit and killed him as it swerved to avoid the jeep. I have to wonder where Rich's ear was tuned as he hopped in his vehicle, fired it up, and sped down the road without a seat belt. What was God saying to Rich at that moment? *"Come spend eternity with me?"* Or, *"RICH: PUT YOUR SEAT BELT ON!!"*

Folks, I am ready to leave this earth someday, but I am not ready to go prematurely. I think we can look at these and others who have gone to heaven early, and let it teach us something about recognizing the voice of God. As I said earlier: *hearing the voice of God is no longer an option.*

While discussions about premature death serve to illustrate a point, perishing can also be a slow process as we fail to grasp all that God has given us through Holy Spirit. The provisions of God through His Spirit are not gifts in the sense of getting nice things to cheer us up. Rather, it is about receiving vital provisions: spiritual ammunition, intelligence, instructions. It's about thriving through proper reinforcements: the word we need, the grace (power) we need, the knowledge and insights required for our survival and perseverance. Holy Spirit is not an option. He is our vital link to life.

The opposite of perishing is growing. Few of us will ever finish growing while here on earth. (Personally, I think the few who did finish were whisked away before they could mess up the rest of us.) Like most people, I am acutely aware of how far I have to grow in God. But my heart is set on reaching my goals and coming to that place of fulfillment. I'm not going to lose sight of the work that He did on the cross, nor the power of His resurrection, nor the life He has given me. Neither am I going to perish as a result of making wrong decisions. He has given me a heart, a mind, and a spirit: HIS SPIRIT! I intend to use those fully to lead the life I am called to live, in Jesus' name. I embrace His grace—that divine empowering leading me to do all things—and I will accomplish that which God is calling me to do.

I'm not saying I never make mistakes; I do! But I take heart in the example of Peter. When Jesus called Peter out of the boat, Peter didn't understand everything that was going on. He just trusted God. Let us do the same: moving from the place where we have to have everything figured out, to the place where we simply and fully trust God. I realize we just talked about some tragic mistakes which Christians have made, but I have learned that there are some mistakes which God expects us to make as He reveals our hearts for growth. When a coach puts a basketball team on the practice court for the first time, does he expect them to play perfectly? No. In fact, if he is a smart coach, he will stage the practices so that most mistakes get made on the practice court. That way, they can be corrected before the real game.

Like Peter, we might sink when we step out, but Jesus will reach down and haul us out as we reach up. I believe the water reached

Peter's legs before he yelled. That's OK. It's when it covers our necks that we need to start worrying (or start swimming). But Peter finished well at the end of his life, according to scripture. So he must have learned a thing or two along the way. We will finish well too, according to scripture. Every one of us will do well, even those who left here before their time. We have their examples. Let us learn from the mistakes which cost them so dearly. Let us not perish but grow.

3rd Promise: Never Separated From God

The third promise of John 10:27-28, is that we will never be separated from God. Reading carefully, it says: *neither shall anyone snatch them out of My hand.* The hand of God includes the provision of God. As we discussed earlier, the provision of God is not given to delight us; it is our vital link to growth and survival. If we learn to recognize the voice of God, we will have all we need. Amen!

Now, these are easy things to say (especially in a book), but I have lived what I am teaching.

In 2003, we were going through a very difficult time in our ministry. My wife was the bookkeeper and she was concerned about our cash-flow. I was not home much during that time. I traveled three weeks of every month that year. At this particular time, I had just come home to grab some clothes and leave again. My wife managed to grab my attention long enough to tell me her concerns. We were in need, she said, and to make it through the next three months, we needed $21,000. At that time, I did not have $21,000. I might have had $21, but not the rest of the zero's.

Well, I took to heart what she said, and as I was driving down the highway on my way to my next engagement, God spoke.

He said, *"It is there."* That was it.

Since my goal in life is to be like God, I picked up my cell phone (after pulling safely to the side of the road), dialed Susan, and said:

"It is there."

Now, you have to understand Susan; she's the practical one. She's the one balancing the books, making both ends meet every month. I'm the one traveling around, doing my thing, praying for people in Wal-Mart and trying to please God.

"What's there?" said Susan.

"God says IT'S there."

"Well, you need to go back and talk to God because I need to know WHAT'S there."

"I don't know what's there, but He said it's there."

I heard the phone click, so I went back to driving. But before I got much farther down the road, she called me back, yelling:

"It's there!"

"What's there?"

"Our money!"

Apparently, soon after God had spoken to me, a man who had never given into the ministry in all the years he had known us, sold a car and sent Susan a check for nearly $22,000.00. *It was there!*

When we listen to the voice of God, we are never separated from His provision. It doesn't always arrive the instant we think it should, but God always comes through. He'll do that for us. He'll do anything abundantly above anything we can ask.

Keep in mind that God's provisions are intended to make us wise Christians, not dependant Christians. There is a difference, and that difference is wisdom. The first month that we need help making our house payment, God will likely help us. The second month, He *might* help us. The third month, expect God to start talking to us about money management, budgetary knowledge, and living within our means. It could be that our needs go way beyond mere cash— most of our needs do. Our needs are often about the exercise of faith, wise handling of money, learning to give and receive, making smart lifestyle choices, and learning to be content with what we have.

Where He guides, He provides. His provision, however, reaches beyond our immediate vision. Sometimes we don't get what we thought we needed. In these times, we have to seek Him in greater measure for the deeper understanding leading to His will for our life. Sometimes we get something completely different than we expected. God gives according to His wisdom, not according to our expectations. If we ask for a new car and He gives us a canoe, guess what? A flood is coming! (Just to be safe, tie the canoe to the roof where you can get to it!)

God is good. His goodness requires growth to fully receive it, and it encourages our growth towards Him. As we learn the voice of God, we will never be separated from the provision of God.

Chapter 3

From the Charismatic to the Spiritual

Years ago, after preaching for many hours at a city-wide meeting in Vancouver, BC, I lay across a bed, tired but fulfilled, and heard Holy Spirit say, *"Would there be a question you want to ask?"* I thought for a long time, considering His offer. This was obviously a one-shot deal. I wanted to ask the best question I could. Finally, I said, *"Where is the church and where are You taking it?"* This is what He spoke to me: *"I'm shifting the church from the charismatic to the spiritual."*

For the past 50 years, the outpouring of God's spirit in America has been experienced largely through the Charismatic movement. While remarkable in many aspects, this movement has been more about temporal spiritual events than lasting spiritual substance. Spiritual events create a mind-set that the next meeting, outpouring, or revelation will dramatically change our lives and solve all our problems forever. Spiritual substance, on the other hand, requires and fosters a deep maturation, an awareness of others, and a sustained relationship with the living God who is seeking to move through our lives.

God is saying we must change our event mind-set and become spiritual people who live, breath and have our being in Him. To do this, we must understand how Holy Spirit equips the saints for the deeper work of God.

Spiritual events don't solve problems; real solutions require work and growth. We all want the miracle cure—and sometimes a miracle is what we need—but the balanced Christian life involves sowing and reaping, challenge and growth, works and rewards, life and death. Somehow there has been a disconnect between earthly living and spiritual life. While the Charismatic outpouring pulled people into churches and re-introduced Holy Spirit in a non-religious setting, it did little for the maturation of the people, which is why Charismatic people—and by association, all Christians—acquired a reputation for being flaky and flighty.

Life is filled with problems; walking with God is filled with answers. The Christian life is not skipping across lily pads of presumptuous "faith." More often, it is dredging the pond to remove a rotting carcass poisoning our water supply.

Grace

> *There are diversities of gifts, but the same Spirit. There are differences of ministries, but the same Lord. And there are diversities of activities, but it is the same God who works all in all. But the manifestation of the Spirit is given to each one for the profit of all.* (1 Corinthians. 12: 4-7)

As we discussed previously, there is one gift: Holy Spirit, and there are diversities of the manifestation of Holy Spirit. A good way to understand the manifestations is to see them as different graces. Now, grace is not merely the unmerited favor of God. Grace is God's empowering of people for specific endeavors. As a result, there are many different graces or empowerments. Let me give you an example from my early days of parenthood.

Susan and I have three children who are now grown. When they were infants and one of them would cry, Susan would say, *"Oh, she's hungry."* She would feed the baby and all was well. Later, the baby would cry again and Susan would say, *"She's wet."* One fresh diaper later and there was peace in the valley. Hours later, the same child would vent her lungs and my wife would say, *"Oh, she wants to be held."* Cradling that child in her arms, I would see the union of peace spreading over baby and mother like a loving blanket. And it occurred to me: Why can't I do that? To me, every cry sounds like: *"I need Momma!"* With mothers, it's different. They have a certain grace and functional authority for babies that I don't have.

Now, to be fair, it's different for me when I'm listening to my Harley. I can tell when the timing needs adjusted, the spark plugs need changed, or the fuel-injectors need cleaned. My wife really doesn't pick up any of this when she rides with me. She just sits back and enjoys the ride.

In the Kingdom of God, all believers are a team—a much larger team. Our strengths vary: they may be in the areas of preaching, teaching, prophesying, business, prayer, education, government, arts, entertainment, media, or science. Some of us can quote ancient Greek while others could care less. The same person who falls asleep on prayer night will be up for three days handing sandwiches to the poor. The prophet who cuts through people's masquerades and sears their hearts might be useless in long-term counseling situations. Mercy and judgment rarely flow from the same cup. But when the Body of Christ comes together to meet needs, God's grace flows in unified abundance.

God gives grace to empower us to be who He's called us to be. Interestingly, God has called us "human beings," not "human doings." The church has been so big on the "doing" part that we've missed the "being" part. Before we can "do," we have to "be." Our "doing" flows out of who we are. When what we do runs counter to what God would have us do, we cannot simply change our "doing." We must change our "being." Often, the problem is that we will not—or cannot—face who we truly are.

I was born-again at 28 years of age, but I was prophetically motivated all my life. I was born with a prophetic call on my life even though I did not yield to it—having been raised in a non-Christian home. I did not yield to my true calling until I became born again and allowed Holy Spirit to make great changes inside of me. But I was always prophetic in nature: I thought in terms of black and white. I was difficult to be around at times. Mercy fled from my presence like water rolling off a hot iron. Ask my wife. On second thought, don't ask my wife.

My dad—who was born again at 63 years of age—had one of the greatest discernment natures of any man I've ever known. He had it before he was saved. As a boy, I'd watch salesmen, who had never met him before, approach our business. Dad would say, *"We're not buying anything from him."* I'd say, *"Daddy, he hasn't even come in yet. What's the deal?"* He'd say, *"I'm not buying from him 'cause he's going to be a liar."* And he'd be right, which is probably why

I grew up telling the truth. It was no use trying to lie to a man who could see right through people.

Later in life, as I got a little theology under my belt, I read:

For the gifts and the calling of God are irrevocable.
(Romans 11:29)

This means that God's gifts and callings are for life, regardless of our spiritual condition. So the unsaved Evangelist is the person at the party getting everybody to do the electric slide. The undeveloped Apostle is the kid in High School organizing fund-drives to sell chocolates to overweight couch potatoes so he can help starving third-world kids. And the confused Missionaries are those who are never comfortable in one place for very long and don't know why.

The answers to "who we are" and "why we are" come when we find out "whose we are." Then we will be equipped to move from isolated, charismatic events of spiritual manifestation to the renewal prophesied in Joel:

And it shall come to pass afterward
That I will pour out My Spirit on all flesh;
Your sons and your daughters shall prophesy,
Your old men shall dream dreams,
Your young men shall see visions.
And also on My menservants and on My maidservants
I will pour out My Spirit in those days. (Joel 2:28-29)

We are living in a day when God is pouring out His Spirit in greater measure. We need to be ready for our traditions to change.

Years ago, my wife and I were trying to rent a house. The landlord knew I was a pastor starting a new church, and he had some questions. Where did I work? What church was I affiliated with? How good was my credit? I told him I was non-denominational and my credit was as good as the Lord's. Well, that wasn't good enough for him.

He asked, *"You're not Baptist or Methodist? Who do you follow?"*

I said, *"The captain of the hosts is Jesus and I'm following in His footsteps."*

Well, that really messed him up. He finally said, *"Well, I go to the United Methodist, but I don't care much for this united stuff."*

Traditions evolve and we must change. Much of the modern Charismatic movement has roots in the Methodist church; that was where the shouting came from. Much of our music has come from Jewish roots, and our greatest hymns have traditional origins.

The Charismatic movement took Holy Spirit out of a staid, religious setting, and introduced Him to non-religious people with very few pre-conditions. As God moves us deeper into the things of the Spirit, we will see Him reaping the best of every movement and folding them into a church united, strong and mature.

As we mature, we must develop a healthy balance between heavenly things and earthly things. It is too easy to get caught up in one realm and neglect the other because people often have an inclination towards one at the expense of the other. I love the spiritual, whereas my wife is very practical. She keeps me balanced. I work very hard to stay tethered to the earth. But I love being spiritual to the point of being spooky. I have to be careful what I manifest and where I do it. Some folks are OK with it; others run from it. I know a church where they love the manifestation of the spiritual. The apostle there actually says, *"I want you to come and be spooky."* I love the spiritual realm, but I don't stay there. I need both sides to live a healthy life.

For some people, the spiritual realm comes easier, while others—the more practical types—struggle with it. Errors and strife come when the two types begin to fight one another.

"Why don't you get a job instead of praying all day?"

"Why don't you help me press-in and get a breakthrough on our finances?"

"Well, while you were praying, I was washing clothes."

"Well if you were more spiritual, we wouldn't have dirty clothes."

47

While these are classic dichotomies, this strife goes beyond the basic division of spiritual-minded people vs. earthly-minded people. The understanding of God's diverse appointments is necessary to understand how we are intended to work together.

> *For we know in part and we prophesy in part....* (I Corinthians 13:9)

When Jesus spoke these words (Matthew 5:48):

> *"Therefore you shall be perfect, just as your Father in heaven is perfect,"*

...He was not addressing an individual. He was addressing an assemblage of believers: His disciples—the first church on earth. His command to be perfect was not directed towards individual perfection but to a corporate perfection. The application of His words echo to us today: *Church: Be perfect, even as I am perfect.* Perfection comes not when individuals are perfected, but when individuals are united and working in harmony. This means individuals of all personalities, persuasions, and perspectives.

I am good at some things but terrible at others—even important things. That is one reason I need people working with me. For example, I have learned much about the spiritual realm, but I have yet to learn how double-entry bookkeeping works. Thankfully, my accountant has this skill and she is vital to our ministry, for she keeps me out of prison. While I admire the Apostle Paul—who spent most of his ministry days locked in a dungeon—I have no desire to do the same. You can't ride Harleys in prison. (Well, you could, but you could only go about 10 feet, then you'd have to turn around.) So while I thank God for my spiritual inclination, I further thank God for the grace on my accountant, my wife, my staff, and the thousands of technical people who keep me straight and enable this great outreach of God to the world. It takes all kinds.

I have learned that the spirit realm is not something we step into or out of like a shower. Nor does the presence of God enter the room when we push the right buttons in worship. God's presence is always with us. What changes is our awareness of it. God doesn't become any stronger when we worship; we simply focus on

His presence which is already there. The first thing to change as we move into the spirit is our perception of the spiritual realm. Often, we pray for God to show up when it is we who must turn our hearts to address the realm in which God waits patiently for us.

God's Grace In Prophecy

The commonly understood words of Joel 2:28 are:

And it shall come to pass afterward, that I will pour out my spirit upon all flesh; and your sons and your daughters shall prophecy....

However, there is a small but important error in most translations. The original text actually reads:

*And it shall come to pass afterwards that I will pour out my spirit on all flesh **as** your sons and daughters prophesy, **as** your young men see visions.*

So we see here a condition to God pouring out His spirit. He will do it *as* we prophesy.

People who operate in this manifestation know from experience that an outpouring of God's spirit accompanies the act of prophesying. However, they sometimes get the order reversed. We can wait for the outpouring of the spirit and then prophesy, or we can prophesy and experience an outpouring of God's spirit. Personally, I'd rather not wait.

We should also examine our motives for prophesying. The fundamental component to prophecy is not speaking for God. Prophecy is hearing from God first, speaking for God second. When we get this order right, the things we prophesy will come to pass, and they will happen as we speak. I have heard very accurate prophecy about certain events, and I have heard inaccurate, skewed prophecy where the person speaking obviously heard or saw something in the spirit, but through a misplaced zeal, put a different spin on it than God intended. This became evident when the events finally came to pass and were nothing of the scale which the prophecy said they would be. For example, I've heard prophecies of huge earthquakes which, when they actually happened, barely registered on the Richter scale. Putting a personal spin on God's words is often a result of immaturity; the person giving the word gets excited because they see something and over-dramatize it.

I have also seen ministers who sought a word from God so they could feel good about themselves over the fact that they prophesied. This is unfortunate. If we need to feel good about ourselves, we should go home to our prayer closet and spend time with God. Our affirmation should come from our relationship with God, not from our level of ministry.

When we accurately hear God, the things we speak will come to pass in the manner in which we describe them. We need to accurately hear and plainly speak God's words. Let us deal with our own agendas in private.

Chapter 4

The Many Ways God Speaks to Us

Then He said, "Go out, and stand on the mountain before the LORD." And behold, the LORD passed by, and a great and strong wind tore into the mountains and broke the rocks in pieces before the LORD, but the LORD was not in the wind; and after the wind an earthquake, but the LORD was not in the earthquake; and after the earthquake a fire, but the LORD was not in the fire; and after the fire a still small voice. (II Kings 19:11-12)

In this verse, Elijah was seeking a word from God and learning an important lesson in the process. God—the master of all earthly elements—chose to inhabit a still small voice in speaking to Elijha. And Elijah—the mighty prophet, the conduit of God's power, the slaughterer of the prophets of Baal—had to find the still, small place in his being in order to hear God. God leads us by the way He speaks to us.

God still speaks in a still small voice today. But that's not the only way that He speaks. He speaks in many ways, and we are going to look at some of those ways in this chapter.

Audibly

When we talk about God speaking, many people think of an audible voice. In fact, God speaking audibly is a very rare occurrence. When it happens, it brings a dramatic life-change to the hearers. Further, when we hear the audible voice of God, we do not just hear it with our ears. When God has spoken audibly to me, I have heard Him in every particle of my body. I heard Him in my toe nails, my hair fissures, in every pore of my body. I find myself radically changed after an experience like that. When God speaks audibly, it penetrates our entire being and we are never the same.

Dreams

God speaks through dreams, reaching our inner-man while our outer-man rests. In sleep, our conscious mind—the center of logic, reason, our daily "churn"—is subdued, and we are more open to the spiritual realm. Because dreams occur in our subconscious mind, many dreams seem bizarre or disjointed. The messages in dreams often transcend time. Some are for the present, some are for the future, and some help us understand the past.

It is important to note that all dreams are not communication from God. Some are simply our mind cleansing itself, processing daily occurrences and filing away memories to make room for further memories. Some dreams are from the pepperoni pizza we had for dinner, others from the novel we read just before bed. When God speaks through dreams, the impressions are lasting, even haunting, until we fully understand and act on that which He has deposited in our being.

I had a reoccurring dream for many months. I was carrying a bucket of liquid gold in my left hand. Then one night, I dreamed I was carrying it in my right hand. After much prayer, I decided that it represented Moses coming down off Mt. Sinai and seeing Aaron and the children of Israel dancing around the golden calf they had made. In his fury, Moses ordered them to beat the false idol into dust. In every church I have been a part of, we have worked hard to remove—beat into dust—the works of man which stood in the way of God. I came to understand this dream as a confirmation in this work.

There are many things we do in church that are merely works designed by man. These works bring about a higher level of activity, but they do not bring about more of God's presence. God seeks to deploy us into activities which establish His will on Earth, but our activities must be rooted in Him. We must be deployed from His presence and our accountability must reach back to Him.

Understanding Godly dreams can be a long-term process. The answers may not come to us immediately, which is why it is important to write down our dreams. When we journal our dreams (the Godly dreams, not the pizza dreams) we can review them later as the issues involved develop further and events transpire. In our crowded, hurry-up-and-wait lives, it is important to keep a record of the things that God shows us during the "night visions."

Visions

Closely related to dreams are visions. Generally, we are awake for these (unless the preacher is really boring). In my experience, there is a distinction between open visions and closed visions. An open vision is something we see external to our being. It seems to be "in the air," like watching a video screen. A closed vision is something we see in our mind. Both are equally important to God.

Visions are powerful tools used by God to lead us. Many times, I've been in prayer to prepare for a service and God has shown me the entire service in a vision. I mean specific things like: *"Lady in the green dress, come up, it's time for God to heal you."* When God confirms our pathway like that, it is a tremendous boost to our faith.

Unction

Ever have an unction? Something stuck in your gut that wouldn't leave you alone until you acted on it? An unction is a strong idea or desire to do something which you can't explain. I had an unction a few years ago to go to a certain store. I didn't know why. I just thought that I was supposed to go to this store. It was a clear, cold day; one of those days when I like to stay around the house eating chili, drinking coffee, and catching up on my reading. But I just felt I had to go, so up out of my easy-chair I rose, grabbed my truck keys, and headed to the store.

Now, for the past few weeks, there had been a negative email campaign going on against me. It was stirring people up and hurting the work we were trying to do in the area. Well, as I walked into the store, I ran into the very person responsible for the emails. It was a bit awkward at first, but we ended up talking it all out, and God began to heal the breach between us, right there in the store. I knew then the reason God led me to that store.

Unctions don't always make sense at the time, but they are one more way for God to lead us by faith.

Impressions

An impression is an unction which doesn't leave a lasting impression—it will go away if we ignore it. An example of this is during worship services when we get an idea to reassure or encourage somebody. If we don't act on it, the moment passes and our thoughts move on to something else.

Personally, I think these are times when Holy Spirit is brooding over a congregation, sending out impressions of things He wants to do. He might say, *"Comfort,"* and twenty people will get the impression that they should go and comfort somebody. So they'll ask themselves who they know who might need comforting, and based in that knowledge or their level of discernment, they might go over and reach out to a person. Or they might not. The moment passes. And next, Holy Spirit may be saying, *"Repentance,"* and five people will drop to their knees in the midst of worship and repent silently before their God. Personally, I'm waiting for Holy Spirit to say, *"Harley,"* and seven of us will mount up and go riding for the day! Silently of course, so as not to disturb the others.

Peace and Joy

Isaiah tells us that we will *"go out with joy, and be led out with peace...."* (Isaiah 55:12) In determining whether I am really hearing God, I have learned to look for His true peace and joy while considering an action. If I find His peace, I am assured that I have heard from God correctly and I have confidence to act. When I don't sense His peace and joy, I hold back, continuing to seek Him until I fully understand what is driving me. When we are truly led by God, His peace and joy are present in a deep, beyond-reason manifestation.

I once carried $200,000 USD into Romania to build 40 churches. It was given by a man who was stationed there in World War II. God had spoken to him saying, *"I'll send you back one day as a blessing."* He gave the money as a fulfillment of that word.

But the operation didn't go smoothly. We were stopped by the police in Bucharest and held for several hours. The whole time, I had the $200,000 divided between two suitcases which were handcuffed to my wrists for security. Now, the police in Romania are not like police in America. The police there are dangerous, underpaid rouges *rogues* who can smell a dollar for a mile. They will kill you for the change in your pocket and feed your body to the buzzards. Our lives were in danger and we were getting nowhere with our detainers. However, the entire time I sat there, I had deep, abiding peace. Finally, I heard the voice of the Lord saying: *"Bribe them."*

Now, that may seem strange to our religious minds. (We all have one; I'm working hard to get rid of mine!) But I can attest that after several hours in a hostile interrogation room with $200,000 strapped to sweating arms, the religious mind is pretty much useless! Besides, what makes more sense? Give those guards $50 apiece and live to build 40 churches holding three services a day, or take a bullet through the brain and have them strip the briefcases from my corpse? So I gave the police $50 each and amazingly, we were on our way.

Unfortunately, my peace was short lived. They walked us out of the interrogation station and towards the plane waiting to take us on the last leg of our journey. Gas was leaking out of the plane and the pilot was standing there smoking! That's when I lost it! The police didn't scare me. The guns didn't scare me. But I'm a pilot, and this situation violently arrested my security! So I gripped my faith, reminded myself that God had sent me, got on the plane, and we arrived in one piece. Praise God!

Now, at this point, some readers may question the difference between this situation and that of Keith Green (which I discussed in chapter 2). The primary difference was that I had received several specific words from God as I proceeded on this mission. God told me to bribe the police so that I could board the plane. He also told me specifically to board the plane. In contrast, I do not think Keith Green received any such word before his plane was overloaded and crashed.

Overloading a plane on a hot and humid East Texas day is a violation of the law of gravity. Smoking in a cockpit is a calculated risk. It is certainly unwise, but even at that time, it was allowed by FAA. Thankfully, God has the final ruling. Keith made a fatal assumption. I prayed and heard God, which brought faith and grace to accomplish His mission.

When we finally reached our destination and laid the money at the feet of the local apostles, it was worth every bead of sweat to be a part of the great move of God in Romania. God told me to go, and He took care of me. The whole time we were detained, I had total peace. It didn't look good from the outside, and I'll confess that my mind wasn't in total peace. But in times of stress, the mind is usually the last place that peace resides. I had peace deeper than my mind. I knew we were going to be OK. I've gone back there several times since. There is a tremendous move of God growing in that region. The police are getting a little nicer, too.

Heart Desires

Scripture says that God speaks through the desires of our heart. Psalms 37:4 tells us:

> *Delight yourself in the Lord and He shall give you the desires of your heart.*

Contrary to popular belief (especially in America), this does not mean that God is going to give us ALL that we desire. I don't know about you, but I can dream fast and big.

The more accurate understanding of this verse is that God *plants* desires in our hearts. To do this, He cultivates our hearts, making them pliable, malleable, and ultimately fruitful. Our desires become His desires. We reap what He sows. The fruit of our lives, realized through fulfillment of our desires, comes from our union with God.

"Behold, a sower went out to sow." (Matthew 13:3)

Voice of Authority

God speaks through the voice of authority. It's a recognizable voice within a voice. It is the difference between a greeting of *"Good morning, Clay,"* and a declaration of *"You WILL have a good morning, Clay!"* The first one is a casual greeting. The second is a positive declaration such that I'd expect storm clouds to part and the heavens to open when I heard it. The first greeting garners my attention and no more. The second—the voice of God's authority—causes me to stand up straight and EXPECT good to come of my morning. It is a clarion call to greatness, if you will, and it requires my obedience if I am to walk in its blessing. Let me give you an example of what I'm describing.

Fourteen years ago, I had a dream about meeting a man named Jack. In the dream, he told me that he had been given a church and that I was the man he had been looking for to take responsibility of the church. This set the stage for a series of things God did to bring us to plant <u>The CityGate at Southaven Church</u>, my present church in Southhaven, Mississippi.

Within 12 months of the dream, I met a man in Florida named Jack, but nothing happened to really connect us. Later, I ran into friends who attended a church in Southaven, Mississippi. They explained that their church was under the oversight of this man, Jack. I was amazed and excited.

During the same trip, a prophet prophesied to Susan and me that we would be moving. At this time of my life, I had the world by the tail. I was traveling to minister three weeks of every month. I had a prospering charismatic ministry, good friends, the favor of God, and a sense that I was changing the world. But I had begun to tell Susan, *"There's one more church to plant."* Every time I said this, she would ask, *"Why?"*

Well, I have learned to wait on God. Part of that discipline is to wait on my spouse. I don't do anything big unless she and I are in agreement. From her response whenever I brought it up, I could tell she wasn't onboard with another move and church plant.

Then one morning in Caldwell, Idaho, Susan woke up before dawn—which was unusual because she's not an early riser. But I could tell by her breathing that she was not sleeping.

"You awake?" I asked.

"Yes," she replied.

"What are you doing awake? You're not sick, are you?"

"No," she said, *"Clay, I want to go down to Southaven and plant a church."*

I heard God's voice of authority in her voice. God had moved on her and she was voicing her desire as well as His desire. I knew that we were headed to Mississippi. It has been a blessing every since.

One comment on agreement before leaving the subject. Many people consider agreement with others to be confirmation that God is leading. Yet nothing could be further from the truth. Agreement is agreement, period. It comes to us many ways. It could mean God is leading but not necessarily. In its essence, agreement means that two or more people are united, period. It does not mean they are right. The disciples were united in the upper room; that was good. But so were the folks building the tower of Babel; they didn't make out so well. A church can be united by Holy Spirit for a work of God or it can be united under a charismatic leader for a work of man. Unity is important, but unity <u>in God</u> is the key. When I heard the authority of God in Susan's voice, I knew we were united in God's will.

When we reach Godly agreement, we fulfill the words of two of my favorite prophets:

> *"Gonna change my way of thinking*
> *Make myself a different set of rules*
> *Gonna put my good foot forward*
> *And stop being influenced by fools."*

(Bob Dylan)

Once we do that, then we can fulfill the second word:

> *"Get 'er done!"*

(Larry the Cable Guy)

Word of God

Of course, most Christians will say that God speaks through the

Bible—and He does. However, gleaning God's voice from the Holy Scriptures is not as simple as it sounds. If it were, then just reading the Bible would solve everybody's problems the world over. Reading the Bible is an excellent place to start, but there is more to hearing from God. Stay with me here for a moment.

There was a word prophesied in Memphis, Tennessee, a few years back that said there was an idol in the mid-south region of the United States (where I presently live), and that idol was the Bible. That word shook some people up! The hate mail flew after that! One guy called and left a raving message:

"Why do you want to teach people how to hear God's voice? Don't you know He's already spoken through His Word?"

Of course, I believe that God has spoken through His word, but I believe He's still speaking today through a variety of means.

The scriptures can be used many different ways. God can speak through them, the flesh can speak through them, even Satan can speak through them. We need to recognize the voice of God which speaks through scripture and in alignment with scripture.

The Bible says that *"faith comes by hearing and hearing by the Word of God."* (Romans 10:17) There are actually three Greek words for the Word of God, but the two we commonly use are *"Logos"* and *"Rhema."* Logos is the written word: what we see on the printed page. Rhema is the God-breathed word: when scripture comes alive in our hearts. I learned this one day as I was reading a familiar scripture and all of a sudden, it jumped off the page and went straight into me! It was the voice of God speaking through His word! When God speaks like that, we suddenly have the faith to step out and do what He is leading us to do. And we have the endurance to finish it.

Meditation

Contrary to some traditional beliefs, meditation is not a sure ticket to the devil. Meditation is mentioned in the Bible and refers to an intense internalization of a scripture or thought. Sure, other groups use it to less-than-Godly ends, but the fault lies with their aims, not their means.

I learned to recognize the voice of God through meditating on a single scripture—John 8:32:

> *And you shall know the truth and the truth shall make you free.*

For twelve months, I meditated on this scripture until God began to speak. I learned to recognize God's voice by believing that I heard Him and then stepping out in faith, repeating what He said and asking Him: *"Did I miss it?"* This didn't start out perfectly; I missed Him a few times. But I learned to pick myself up and work with a safety-net under me so that if I did fall, I'd be OK and nobody else would get hurt. I learned that if the voice I thought was God led me and those around me into greater freedom, I could take this as confirmation and build from there. But if it led us to bondage, it was obviously not God and I needed to figure out where I missed Him.

Ways God Doesn't Speak

Here are some ways that God prefers <u>not</u> to speak.

As we mature in Him, we will find that God prefers to not speak through circumstances. Circumstances can just as often go against us as for us. We simply can't base our determination of God's will on the flow of circumstances. If I would have lived by the circumstances over the past five years, I would have never stayed to see my present church planted or prospering.

Now certainly there is a balance to this. I had a friend who told his wife that he was going down the road to get a paper. After he left, she switched on the TV and saw a live news bulletin about a car driving the wrong way on the freeway. Alarmed, she called her husband to warn him.

"Be careful!" she said. *"There's a car driving the wrong way on the freeway."*

"One car?" he said. *"There's hundreds of them!"*

We have to know where God has placed us, where He is leading us, and where He expects us to remain. If every car is a missile heading straight towards us, we should at least check that we are on the road God has for us. If we are, we should keep driving and not let the circumstances deter us. If we are not, we need to get things straight.

Similar to walking by circumstances, God prefers to not speak through fleeces. They were a tool of the old covenant. In our new covenant relationship with God, people who put out fleeces end up getting fleeced. Why do we need a fleece to know what we should do in our everyday lives? Even simple things like whether to pray for an extra hour are sometimes determined by a fleece. Sound strange? I know people who pray that way. They seek a sign to do something which, deep down inside, they know to do anyway. Why not just pray another hour? God speaks today. Why not step out and do what is in our hearts? Why do we think we need fleeces? Are we trying to rationalize not moving from our comfort zones? Remember, His will is planted in our hearts. We need to act on our Godly desires and know that He will honor our motives.

Finally, God prefers to not lead individuals through personal prophetic words. Now, this might sound strange coming from me. I've traveled in 57 nations as a prophet of God, spoken words over multitudes of people, and received feedback from many on how these words impacted their lives. But I firmly believe God prefers not to lead people through prophets if He can help it. In the charismatic and prophetic groups I've been a part of, we have developed a tendency to seek prophetic words for everything. But this is not scriptural, it's not balanced, and it's not healthy. The very reason I teach on hearing the voice of God is for the Body of Christ to hear God for themselves. We cannot succeed in the coming move of God if we are dependent on the voice of a prophet for our personal leading. At best, personal prophecy should be for confirmation or guidance, supporting what God has already told us or alerting us to things we do not see. Prophecy which leads us to major life changes should always be confirmed before acting on it. In the end, we walk by the Word of God, not by the word of the prophet.

Interesting Prophecies

Since I made the bold statement that God prefers not to lead individuals through prophetic words, I'd like to share some of the more interesting prophecies I have given people—all with good results.

I was in a meeting in Pine Bluff, Arkansas, when the Lord gave me a word for a woman in the congregation. I called her to the front and told her: *"The Lord says He brought you to this city for the Scarecrow, the Tin-man and the Lion."*

Now that was weird, wasn't it? What was I doing prophesying about characters from the The Wizard of Oz? But that was the word I had, so I gave it.

After the meeting, the lady came up to me and said, *"You're not going to believe this, but…"*

I said, *"Lady, I've been doing this so long, I'll believe anything."*

She said, *"Well, number one: I just moved from Kansas, my name is Dorothy (meaning gift of God) and God told me to move here.*

And number two: He told me when I got here, that I was to pray that people would have a heart change and receive a heart after God, that they would get the mind of Christ, and that they would find the courage to fulfill their destiny."

I recalled that in the Wizard of Oz, the Tin-man sought a heart, the Lion sought courage, and the Scarecrow sought a brain. So it all made sense. It is experiences like this which have taught me to give the word I hear from God without changing it to fit my limited understanding.

God will use anything to jar our consciousness. Early one morning, I was lying in bed next to my darling wife. It was about 6:00 AM, and I heard an old song from the 60's:

> *"What goes up, must come down.*
> *Spinning wheel, got to go round."*

I nudged Susan.

"Do you want to know what the Lord just said to me?"

"No. I want to sleep," she said drowsily.

"The Lord just said:

> *'What goes up, must come down.*
> *Spinning wheel, got to go round.'"*

I could tell she was overwhelmed—the snoring gave her away. But this word really shook me. We had a woman leave our church recently because she and her husband couldn't take the correction they were given. They left very mean-spirited. The last thing she said as she walked out the building was: *"I'll NEVER have anything to do with you and this church again!"* That morning, thirty minutes after hearing God speak, she called me crying because her husband had just left her and she needed our help. Spinning wheels came around.

Here's another example—probably the strangest and most unique word I ever gave anybody.

I was ministering at a church service one Sunday night. I had about 200 people in a prayer line when I heard Holy Spirit say to me, *"Tell this woman she's been living a lie, but the lie is alright."*

My religious mind went *"tilt, tilt, tilt, tilt!"* So I stood there a few minutes. Then I heard God say it again: *"Tell her she's living a lie, but the lie is alright."*

In my super-spiritual persona, I decided to stand my ground, muttering: *"Get behind me, Satan!"* That's when I heard Holy Spirit say emphatically: *"Son, I SAID TO TELL HER: she's living a lie, but the lie is alright."*

When God gets to that point, there's no mistaking His voice, so I turned to the pastor of the church and said, *"I have a very peculiar word for this lady."* He had traveled several times with me, so he knew how strange I could be when I operated in the prophet's authority (not just the prophetic realm).

He said, *"Don't tell me. Tell her."*

So I stood before her and said: *"The Lord says to tell you: you are living a lie, but the lie is alright."*

The woman fell to the floor and cried uncontrollably.

Later, after she recovered, she told us her story. As she talked, it was obvious that she had led a hard life. I would have guessed her age as 55 years before she fell and cried, but after she arose with this great burden lifted, she looked as if she was only 40. Turned out, there was evidence against her husband who was part of a drug cartel. She was in the witness protection program so she wouldn't be killed. She said she felt that she was living a lie and that she shouldn't be in church under those conditions, especially serving in any capacity. The word I gave her relieved her greatly, changed her life, and made her free from all condemnation. My narrow religious mind almost cheated that woman out of a word that changed her life.

Hopefully, we can see from this chapter that God is still speaking today and that He speaks in a variety of ways. Do not limit God. Be sure you understand who you are hearing and following. It is with great caution that scripture reminds us of our enemy's various disguises. In the following chapters, we will learn the attributes of God's voice and the enemy's voice.

When the truth is understood, there can be no confusion.

Chapter 5

Attributes of the Voice of the Enemy

Many years ago, God told me something about His voice and the voices in opposition to Him.

The voice of God silences the voice of the enemy and neutralizes the feelings of the flesh.

These words impacted me so deeply that I based my life on learning the voice of God. It has occurred to me since then, that it is just as important to learn the voice of the enemy.

How many of us even believe that the enemy has a voice? If we can accept that the enemy has a voice, is it a far stretch of logic to accept that he wants to disrupt and destroy us with that voice? The first step in that destructive progression is to get us listening to his voice as if it were our own thoughts or those of God. By examining some key attributes of the enemy's voice, we can develop greater discernment.

Pressure

When the enemy speaks, it brings pressure. There is an urgency to his suggestions and demands. He knows that his words cannot stand close examination, so he gets us moving in his direction before we have time to reflect and question whether we are truly hearing from God. Salesmen use a similar tactic. A car salesman will offer you a seemingly great deal, then say the classic words: *"But you have to buy it tonight."* Pressure! Panic! Stop thinking. Sign now!

I know this tactic well: I was a GMC salesman for many years. My specialty was closing deals. I was the guy who popped out of the back room when the regular salesman could not get any further with a prospective customer. The devil wants us to close the deal with him before we walk out of his showroom. He stirs our emotions with a sense of opportunity knocking once. This pressure bears down on our common sense and causes us to act in haste without adequate thought.

The enemy lies to us. The more we listen to the lies, the more powerful the lies become. Sickness often starts out as lying symptoms, then the enemy pressures us with fears of what these symptoms foretell. Soon, we start to believe we are sick and the symptoms grow in severity. We lend credence to the lies and they become real through our own belief.

In 1989, I was in Hattiesburg, Mississippi, preparing to visit Romania with David Sumerall, when strange feelings came over me. I knew immediately where these feelings were coming from. So I spent the night fighting off the symptoms of a heart attack. It was a major battle which my God won! Had I bought in to the lies and let fear enter my heart, I would have empowered the lies and quite possibly experienced the very thing the lies foretold. There is a hereditary tendency towards heart disease in my family, but that is not the heritage I base my life on. I am now of the lineage of Jesus. Last I checked, His heart was just fine. I align myself with Him through faith, which is the act of joining my reality with God's reality through my belief system. It works the same in the negative direction when we align our reality with the world's reality. Our belief system governs our lives.

When we hear things which do not align with God's words, we cannot allow ourselves to be pressured to act. Maybe it is a great deal; maybe it isn't. But I can tell you, 99% of the time, that new truck will still be available in the morning, at an even better price!

Fear and Confidence

The voice of the enemy brings fear, eroding our confidence in ourselves and God. I have learned that people who habitually listen to the enemy have a singular lack of confidence. The enemy promises them things which appeal to their weakened state. In reality, the enemy's lies only serve to further erode their confidence, making them susceptible to greater lies.

Fear is the absence of love. As fear grows inside of us, it displaces God's love. The Bible tells us in I John 4:18: *perfect love casts out fear,....*

God wants us to have confidence, both in Him and in what we can do with Him. Yet there is a fine line between confidence and arrogance. Sometimes arrogant people act that way to mask a lack of true confidence. Other times, people who are brimming with confidence over what their mighty God can do, may appear arrogant.

I'm very confident about what God can do in the realm of the prophetic. I've ministered worldwide in 57 countries. I've prophesied words over nations, regions and churches, and I've watched the promises of the Lord come to pass. That's not arrogance; it's an awareness of the mighty God in my life. I've also been brought low by God when I needed it. I've made mistakes. I've stepped out in mistaken faith into areas He did not want me in. I have learned from those mistakes. I am also humbled by the things I do not know. As I said earlier: I am very strong in the spiritual. I am not so strong in other areas of life. But we all serve a mighty God. It is not arrogance to expect great things to occur in our lives, as long as our expectations are based on the One who created us and now dwells in us.

As corrosive as fear is in the life of a Christian, worse is false humility. While there is a place for humility, true humility is not based on our assumed lack of power. Rather, it is based on an awareness of who we are and whose we are. We should be the best preachers, engineers, salesmen, evangelists, painters, writers, carpenters, bricklayers, accountants, waiters, congress-people, and business-people who ever walked the face of the earth. We should be great because we were made in the image of a GREAT GOD! We are great because He is great. We are the best because He is the best. Anything less is false humility.

This is not to be confused with the pride which precedes a fall (Proverbs 16:18). Destructive pride comes when we forget who made us; when we forget who empowers us. We cannot let the voice of the enemy fool us into thinking that a "nothing" self-image is somehow Godly. God is not "nothing," and neither are we. Let us muster the courage to be who God made us to be, making no apologies for it.

Confusion

The voice of the enemy brings confusion. In my many years of ministry, I have counseled every situation imaginable. A common thread runs through all of them: confusion. I have found that the people listening to the voice of the enemy are confused, and the road of confusion leads to greater confusion. Jesus told us that the truth will set us free. In the strategy of the enemy, he uses confusion to keep people off balance. If we don't know who else to believe or trust, we are most vulnerable to one who seems to offer us a way out. Confusion leads us to accept a leading hand of someone we do not know, desperately trusting where they lead us. The tragedy comes when our unseen guide is our enemy intent on the destruction of all we are, all we love, and all we touch.

Things get worse when we start to believe the subtle lie which says that spiritual matters have no absolutes. If the enemy can get a person to believe that their lives are more spiritual, exciting, fresh and relevant because of the lack of firm guiding principles, they are on the road to ruin. Anyone who has successfully raised a child—I say successfully because it is a very real possibility to fail in this endeavor—will tell you that without clear, guiding principles, that child will grow up a mess and fall into a pit of troubles, confusion being chief among them.

This confusion ought not to be. Spiritual truth is clear: it is Jesus. And many a hallowed page has been written to describe Him for our illumination.

Doubt and Wrong Questions

The voice of the enemy causes us to ask the wrong questions and fail to ask the right questions. Many of us want to ask God why certain things happened. I've come to realize that this can be a very foolish line of questioning. The best question for God is not *"why,"* but what glory He will get out of something.

I once took a call at 2:00 AM from a family who is very dear to us. Their son, Tony, a young man over whom I had prophesied that was to be a pastor, had burned to death in his home. It took my wife and I two hours before we had the strength to drive and meet with this family who had lost their 21 year old son. As we started to drive, I asked God *"why?"* and I received a sharp rebuke: *"Don't ever ask me why!"*

After 15 minutes of stinging silence, I meekly asked, *"Father, what can I ask you?"*

He said, *"Ask me what I am going to do to get the glory."*

At Tony's funeral, we played praise music and his mother worshiped God with total abandon. I preached the gospel and many of his friends came to Tony's casket to accept Jesus. At the cemetery, I spoke again and six more friends gave their heart to Jesus.

I learned that day that when we ask *"why?"* we are playing into the hands of the enemy. It can bring doubt, confusion, and endless, fruitless questions. I do not believe it was God's will for Tony to die. But it happened and God got glory from it because we trusted Him.

Condemnation

When the enemy speaks, it brings condemnation. I find this most prevalent in areas where there is a strong religious spirit, such as the deep-South region of the United States. I once counseled an unmarried young couple who had conceived a child. The young woman, who had been raised in my church, was under strong condemnation. I told her plainly that being pregnant outside of marriage was not a sin. The sin had already occurred, and the pregnancy was the result. The real question was: had they asked God to forgive them? They said they had, so I told her, *"You carry this child free from guilt because God has forgiven you. His Word says that when He forgives sin, He casts it into the sea of forgetfulness."* They left that day much relieved.

Unfortunately, the church doesn't always work this way. The enemy brings condemnation, then convinces everyone that it is God who is doing the condemning. In the end, religious-minded people live under crushing condemnation, made worse by the fear of further condemnation. God's forgiveness is preached in their churches but rarely practiced.

A major factor in bringing people out of this trap is leadership that can be trusted—leaders who understand the full scope of God's forgiveness. I led a church for years before some people finally came to me and confessed things they held inside. When I asked why they waited this long, they replied: *"Now I believe I can trust you."* When people see the unconditional love of God in our lives, they will begin to trust us. Confessing our sins to one another follows the model of God's forgiveness and leaves no grounds for condemnation.

Do not confuse condemnation with conviction; they are not the same. Conviction is from God. It alerts us to sin. As such, it is a necessary step towards cleansing and it always brings life. Condemnation is a stain we can never cleanse, no matter how hard we scrub. It only gets worse and it leads to death.

Thankfully,

> *"There is therefore now no condemnation to those who are in Christ Jesus, who do not walk according to the flesh, but according to the Spirit." (Romans 8:1)*

Weariness

When the enemy speaks, we often feel physically and spiritually drained. While God's words bring life, the enemy's words sap us of strength and the will to move forward. Then when we are worn out, we are much more susceptible to the influence of the enemy.

Many people get caught up in the frantic buzz of being busy all the time. In a healthy life, there is a time for full-on activity and a time for vegetating. The key to healthy activity is found in our core purposes. Busyness without a reasonable purpose is insanity. We often find ourselves busy doing things which really don't need to be done. Rest is something which needs to be done. The fallen super-saints of our present generation who make the news with their spectacular moral failures are often people who drove themselves to the brink of collapse, building empires to the heavens while neglecting their mortal framework. We need time to be refreshed. We need to stop long enough to say, *"What was that again, God? Oh yeah...."* Rising up with wings of eagles as Isaiah promised us, is preceded by waiting on the Lord.

The enemy seeks greater influence over us when we are physically tired and spiritually drained. Part of the enemy's plan is to see us work too hard and too long, paying on debts which only seem to grow. We are susceptible to the enemy when we are weary. Weaknesses which we can normally handle become huge obstacles when we are drained.

We can also find ourselves tired from doing good, and this can be a surprise if we are not prepared for it. Conventional thinking goes like this: we are ministering in the spirit, so we should be full of God's strength in the end, right? Wrong. When we minister, the flow of energy is going from us to the object of our ministry. We must take time to let God minister back to us, replenishing the flow into us. Furthermore, we must learn to minister from the overflow of a full heart.

Labor to enter into His rest.

Job's Friends

Sometimes the enemy's voice comes through Job's friends. Recall that in the book of Job, it was first his friends and then his wife who turned on him and spoke things out of line with God's will.

Fortunately, not all wives are like that. My wife of 36 years is my chief encourager. Job's wife had a different take on things: *"Do you still hold fast to your integrity <Job>? **Curse God** and die!"* (Job 2:9). That's not real encouraging. (I suspect she had some life insurance on him.)

The reason that Paul taught his protégée Timothy to *"commit these to faithful men..."* (2 Timothy 2:2) is that there are some people with whom we should not share the deeper things of our life. Godly words from trusted sources help us align our dreams and visions with God's will. Ungodly words from ungodly people sow seeds of doubt, fear, and darkness into our lives. Agreement is a powerful force which works both ways.

Sometimes the ungodly words are sown outside the church right after the service. The fowls of the air descend upon the parking lot as the talk starts, seeking to pluck the seeds from hearts as people make statements through questions.

"What did you think about the sermon?"

"Have you ever seen such carrying on?"

"Where does she get off, speaking up like that?"

"Do you really believe Brother Roy is an apostle?"

"Do you think Ruth is really called to lead the praise team?"

We must be careful who we listen to, and guard whose words are being sown in our hearts.

Miracles

As we learn to recognize the voice of God, we will see miracles like we have never seen before. I have seen firsthand what God will do if we let Him. I prayed for a lady with a toothache and she got a gold filling with a diamond embedded in it. This was documented by her dentist. In England, George Jeffrey prayed for a man who had been born without eyeballs. George pushed his thumbs in the man's eye sockets and prayed. When he pulled his thumbs back out, the man could see. The reason God does these things is, first of all, to help those afflicted, and second, to demonstrate that He can do anything if we let Him.

Another preacher named Stephen Jeffreys had a lady come to one of his meetings pushing her husband in a wheelchair. He'd had a leg amputated. She rolled him right up to Stephen and told him that he's here to get a leg.

Stephen Jeffreys asked her, *"Did you bring a sock and a shoe?"*

The lady said, *"No, I didn't."*

He said, *"Well, where is your faith? I won't pray for him."*

The next evening, the lady and her husband returned, shook the sock and shoe out in front of Stephen and said, *"We've come in faith tonight!"* He prayed for him and the leg grew out.

I verified this miracle through conversation with Stephen Jeffreys' grandniece. I also talked to Brother Horace Bettney, who was just a boy in that meeting. He saw that leg grow out and he became a preacher because of it. He preached for 60 years and the passion whenever he told this story made it as real as if it happened yesterday. Liars don't lie passionately, at least not for long.

I had the opportunity to sit with a man named Albert Hibbard, who worked with Smith Wigglesworth. Albert died a few years ago. As a young man, Albert Hibbard was walking behind Smith Wigglesworth one day. (He said Wigglesworth would never let him walk beside him, only behind him.) Suddenly Wigglesworth took off running and Albert ran after him. Wigglesworth ran as hard as he could toward a house and hollered through the keyhole in the door, *"Don't do it. God loves you!"* A few moments later, the door opened, revealing a chair, a hangman's noose, and a man who was just about to commit suicide. *"I was there at that door and saw it,"* said Albert. Smith Wigglesworth was in a place to hear God and save a man's life! Seeing God work like that changed Albert Hibbard's life.

Voice of the Flesh

Like the enemy, the flesh never speaks in accordance with God's living Word. Sure, it can quote scripture, but it will twist it, spin it, pervert it: in essence, remove Holy Spirit from it. It does this because God's Word is powerful. The enemy always attacks the areas most vital for our life. The flesh wants to divorce us from the power of God's Word.

Offense

The voice of the flesh incites us to become offended in any personal conflict. The Body of Christ is very immature in this area; we are too easily and permanently offended. We have adopted the prevailing attitude of our society in that we don't deal honestly with our personal conflicts; we simply get offended, erect a barrier, and walk away. Unfortunately, barriers stay up for life unless we consciously take them down. We think we are taking the easy route by separating ourselves from what offends us—and in the short term, we are. But in the long term, we only reap greater difficulties because we never learn to adequately deal with our conflicts. Running from a problem leads us straight into our flesh—our unredeemed man.

We need to realize that being offended is a choice which starts with who or what we choose to listen to. I choose to not be offended because I choose to listen to God rather than my flesh.

The easiest place to become offended is at church. Church is filled with imperfect people, and the more the church grows, the more imperfect it becomes. The Body of Christ should reflect the full personality of her namesake. But often, the best we can do is point to He who is perfect. When churchgoers fail to make the distinction between a faulty body and a perfect Jesus, they fall into the trap of offense and leave the gathering greatly upset, vowing to find another church more to their liking. However, they will not find peace at their next church if they haven't left the last church in peace. Their frustrations, attitudes, and convictions will follow them because of the power of the inner vows which they have made.

We can only enter a place of peace if we have left the last place in peace. This is true in church groups, employment situations, and relationships. We must leave in peace. This means forgiving those who we think wronged us. Leave in peace and we can enter in peace.

Shifting Sand Questions

As the influence of our flesh deepens, it will begin to entrench its power in our lives through a series of open-ended questions designed to steer us away from truth and hold us in a death-spiral. It causes us to ask wrong questions in the face of overwhelming truth. In counseling, I hear this in the form of *"but"* answers to plain truth. I tell people what the Word of God says, and they say:

"But, Apostle..."

"But my situation's different."

"But you don't know my wife."

"But the Bible doesn't apply here."

"But I HAD to!"

The worst place these "but" statements occur is in marriage.

In the early years of our marriage, I had gone away for a month on a duck hunting trip. When I got home, I found a very upset Susan furiously packing her bags. When I asked her what she was doing, she said,

"I can't take it any more. You're gone all the time. All you think about is duck hunting. I'm going home to my Momma's."

So I went to the closet and pulled out my suitcase.

"What are you doing?" she asked.

"Honey, if it's too tough for you, it's too tough for me. I'm not living here without you. If you're going to your Momma's, I'm going to your Momma's, and we'll have dinner there."

Well, she sat down on the bed and started crying. I put my arms around her and we began to talk. In the end, I made a promise to cut out most of my time away from home. When that didn't sway her, I even offered to give up golf.

"But you don't play golf," she said.

"For you, Honey, I'll just have to learn."

That was 32 years ago, and we are still going strong.

The Voice of Flesh is Changeable

When we heed the voice of the flesh, we find it as changeable as the ocean sands. When the flesh speaks to us, it will tell us that we need to do one thing, and as we start to do this, it will tell us to do something else.

Built on these shifting sands, we have two groups in the church today: those who live by preference and those who live by conviction. When we follow the voice of God, it brings faith aligned with His will and causes us to live by conviction. But when we follow the flesh, we live by preference.

"I prefer this church because the worship is good there."

"I prefer that church because they've got a great day-care."

And the best one I ever heard—true story: A man came back from visiting another church and said:

"You've got to go! They've got the best pie I've ever had!"

The voice of the flesh leads us to make choices based on preference, not conviction.

In Genesis, Cain and Abel struggled in the same areas. Abel brought an offering to God out of conviction, whereas Cain brought an offering out of preference. People who live by preference will despise those who live by conviction, rising up and trying to kill them by any means available, including malicious words.

Temporal

The voice of the flesh is temporal in that the passions, dreams, and goals it engenders are shifting, never solid nor enduring. In my years of ministry, it has been common for some passionate person to come to me saying: *"Apostle, the Lord's telling me we need to start a soup kitchen, start feeding the hungry and helping the poor and you know...."* So I have developed this answer: *"Write out for me three pages of your vision, put it on paper, bring it to me, and we'll sit down and start praying over it. Then we'll get behind you and help you do it."*

This is a good test. Roughly 85% of those people never return. I have learned that when the Lord burdens our heart with something, it is enduring; we are not going to escape it. If we can't put it on paper, chances are it's not really there, it's just a phantom that our flesh is throwing up. Sure, every accomplishment starts with a vision, a hope, a passion, but it must mature from there. Psalm 1 tells us that everything the Godly do will prosper and come to maturity. In other words: it will bear good fruit. Not so with the dreams of the flesh, regardless of how noble they may seem in the beginning.

Authority

The voice of the flesh leads us to resist authority. Church splits are the perfect example of this. Churches don't split over doctrine or finances or the length of the choir robes. They split over authority, power struggles, fighting over who is in charge. The church may put a spiritual face on the conflict and say it's about something noble like tongues or baptism or salvation, but really, it's who's in power and who's not.

Rarely does the flesh lead a person to submit to legitimate authority unless there is an ulterior motive. When the flesh does assume a form of submission, it is often done with grumbling, discord, resentment, and plots of revenge and mutiny. Anyone who has raised a teenager can attest to at least a glimpse of this attitude. The flesh is rebellion personified; it willfully submits to no master. Which is why we deal with it resolutely; there can be no compromise. We know we are serving God when we willingly and peacefully submit to Godly authority.

Wise Counsel

The voice of the flesh will lead us away from wise counsel and towards a loner lifestyle. From Proverbs 18:1, we read:

A man who isolates himself seeks his own desire; he rages against all wise judgment.

Isolation is a seductive tool of the enemy. Had Eve not been separated from her husband, I doubt she would have been deceived by the serpent. There's power in agreement. When we listen to our flesh, we do not yield to those in authority. Further, we actively reject those who would counsel us wisely.

My wife and I always make major decisions together. In times past, it was often my decision and her agreement. But we learned from that. Now we pray and seek counsel together to find agreement with what God is saying. That way, when we step out to do something, God comes in and it gets done. Amen!

Chapter 6

Attributes of the Voice of God

In the previous chapter, I focused on ways to recognize the voices of the flesh and the enemy. Endless pages could be filled to describe every nuance and characteristic of these two voices. However, most of us would still be fooled, were it not for one thing: the clear distinction between these imposters and the voice of God.

When banks teach tellers how to spot counterfeit money, they not only teach them the characteristics to look for in fake money, but they also teach their tellers to be experts in the real thing. The goal is to make sure no teller can be fooled by the imposters, no matter how cleverly made. This requires time spent handling real money—feeling it, smelling it, sensing it—until there is complete familiarity with its characteristics.

The trouble with delineating each characteristic of the false voices is that the enemies of God have endless variations on their themes. The old saying rings true here: *The trouble with making anything foolproof is that fools are so ingenious.* When it comes to the enemies of God, they are ingenious in their deception. Hence, it is fruitless to carry the study of counterfeit voices further than the highlights (or "*low* lights") which I have already covered. Instead, if we are to detect the counterfeits of this present age, we must become intimately acquainted with the voice of God Himself. Nothing else will protect us from the tsunami of deceit seeking to carry us away.

As I say throughout this book:

> **The voice of God silences the voice of the enemy and neutralizes the feelings of the flesh.**

Here are some characteristics of the voice of God:

Pressure and Conviction

When God speaks, He rarely puts pressure on us. Pressure is a tool of the enemy. Now, there is a difference between pressure and conviction. God's voice can convict us, but the pressure to act in haste—except in rare situations—does not serve God's purposes. Scripture tells us that God prepares us, His Grace empowers us, and His righteousness qualifies us for the work ahead. The impulse to jump hastily into the unknown is a sign of the enemy's urging, not God's.

Isaiah 52:12 says,

> *"For you shall not go out with haste, nor go by flight; for the LORD will go before you, and the God of Israel will be your rear guard."*

God is watching out for us; He is preparing us. Nothing we do will need to be done in haste. I've learned to wait on God. In the past when I've acted in haste, I've ended up in trouble. See, I tend to run ahead of God. If God begins a sentence, I finish it for Him and rush off to do what I think He was going to say. I suspect that deep down inside, God likes that in me. But more importantly, He knows me and can handle me. Most times, when God wants to tell me something, He first puts me in a position where I can't run off half-cocked. I like that about Him. And I'm working on staying still until I fully understand His will.

When we completely understand His will, there is no need to act impulsively. As the Israelites approached the Red Sea, they may have thought that God failed them in not giving them swimming lessons, but it soon became obvious that He had prepared both them and the environment for their great escape.

Instead of acting in haste, I've learned to depend on a multitude of counselors. I teach the married men in my congregations a novel way to spell "Holy Spirit." It is spelled: W-I-F-E. The best place to hear Holy Spirit is through your Godly spouse. Almost as important are Godly friends and those in authority over your life. Listen to them. I'm not saying to rush out and do whatever they say; that is not the message. The message is to hear and consider the wisdom God places in the voices of those around us. God has a purpose in this: He feeds where He leads. We are not all mavericks. We are a body: strong when united, slaughtered when divided.

We must learn to hear the smallest of voices: the voices of children, the voices of those we deem lower than ourselves, the voices of passersby. God calls us to the places we should be through the voices of those who, in our haste or self-importance, we would otherwise overlook.

A while back, I wanted to buy my first laptop, but I didn't have the money. Lo and behold, a credit card arrived in the mail, one which I never requested.

I told Susan, *"God sent me this credit card so that I can get that laptop."*

She didn't see it that way. *"We better wait until we've got cash to pay for it."*

She was wrong, of course, and I told her so.

Finally, she said plainly, *"If you buy a laptop with that credit card, a curse will come on the laptop."*

Well, I could see I needed go straight to God on this one, since Susan obviously wasn't hearing Him. My prayer went something like this:

"God, I thank you for this credit card—it has a great interest rate. Just think of the great things I could accomplish for you with a laptop."

God said, *"If you buy a laptop with that credit card, it will be cursed."*

I said, *"God, have you been talking to Susan?"*

At that point, it was two against one, so I gave up, saved up the cash and finally got the laptop. Two months later, God told me to give it away to an apostle who needed it. Suddenly, it all made sense. I was glad I wasn't making payments on a laptop I didn't own. Later, I had another laptop given to me. I treasure it more than the first one because of the people who gave it to me. See, I wanted to jump the moment I got that credit card. But God had a better plan and I needed to follow it.

Confusion

The voice of God never brings confusion. Scripture tells us

> *"For God is not the author of confusion but of peace, as in all the churches of the saints"* (1 Corinthians 14:33).

Now, what is confusion to man is not confusion to God. God is NEVER the author of confusion. In the book of Acts, we read:

> *"Some therefore cried one thing and some another, for the assembly was confused, and most of them did not know why they had come together."* (Acts 19:32)

The apostles finally arrived and began working to alleviate the confusion, commending the people to grace. When confusion sets in, God's grace removes it.

God's Character

Psalms 103:7 says,

> *"He made known His ways to Moses, His acts to the children of Israel."*

Many people today struggle with confusion because they know God only from the knowledge of His acts. The problem with this approach is that God can (and does) change how He does things. However, He remains true to His character. In Acts Chapter 5, when Ananias and Sapphira lied to Peter (and to God) about their giving, God struck them dead. Now, I'm certain many of us have lied about our giving at times in our lives, and God in His mercy did not strike us dead (or else you would not be reading this). Instead He led us to correction. I like that. I like it when God does not strike me dead for making mistakes or saying stupid things.

As we come to know the character of God, we establish a strong foundation for recognizing His voice. He never speaks contrary to

His character.

Order

In contrast to confusion and pressure, the voice of God establishes a methodical order. In Isaiah 28:13 it says,

> *"the Word of the Lord was to them, precept upon precept,
> line upon line, here a little, there a little...."*

God can act suddenly, but most of the time He is very methodical in the way that He works. Now, I like it when God acts suddenly.

Me: *Help!!*

God: *WHAM!*

Me: *Cool!*

I also like it when God is consistent. Wes King wrote a song
with the line: *"Slow miracles, are the only kind that will last."* We
often want God to move in upheaval, chaos, and swift destruction
of all our obstacles. Certainly these are the more dynamic aspects of
God—the ones which grab headlines and make great praise songs—
but the lasting transformative works of God are consistent, steady,
sweeping, thorough—characteristics which don't violently arrest
our attention but instead, cause us to lift up our heads one day and
exclaim: *"Oh, look at that. I didn't see you working there, God! Nice
job."*

God can destroy our enemies or He can transform our enemies.
He can tie up our rebellious teenagers and toss them to the jailers until they are old enough to collect social security. Or He can patiently
work on their hearts and in time, make them loving, respectable,
productive human beings. (Yes, He *is* the God of miracles!) We can
throw our malfunctioning laptops out the car window at 90 mph,
or we can call tech support, wait on the line for 3 hours, and... ah,
you get the point. The dynamic gets our attention, but the consistent
changes our lives. When we hear the voice of God, we should expect
it to line up with His consistent, orderly mode of operating.

The Written Word

When God speaks, it always lines up with His written word. He gave us the Bible to guard us against deception and lead us from error. The trouble comes when God speaks things to us which do not line up with our theology. There are things in the Bible which our theology does not allow us to see. This is normal: theologies, like skin, must grow as our insides grow. When God speaks things which challenge us, before we label the voice as "the enemy" because it "doesn't agree with the Bible," we need to take the time to look at what the Bible really says. And we must do it with open hearts and minds. That challenging word could very well agree with the Bible but violate our theology. And when it comes to God or our theology, guess which one wins?

Developing Revelation

When we receive the God-breathed word—the Rhema—we receive a revelation from the word at that moment, but as we position ourselves in obedience to the word, we receive a greater revelation from the same word.

In 1984, God told me, *"I want you to go home and close yourself in a prayer closet for the next five months."* I obeyed, and there were things that God said to me during that time of prayer and Bible study that I thought I understood. But later, as I walked in the revelation He gave me during that time of prayer, I learned in much greater measure the things He first revealed to me. With every step of obedience that I took, there came a greater understanding.

I used to think that when God spoke to me, it was revelation. I've since learned that when God speaks to me, it is first knowledge or information, but after I learn to apply the knowledge and walk in it, it becomes wisdom and revelation. Information without wisdom will just get us into trouble.

I heard about a man who wanted to do something he had never done before. So after reading a book on skydiving, he strapped on a parachute, rode a plane to 12,000 feet, and jumped out. As he fell, he realized his chute was broken. He didn't know anything about fixing parachutes, but since the earth was rapidly approaching and his options were limited, he took off the parachute and tried to fix it himself. The wind was ripping past his face and he was dropping like a rock. At 5,000 feet, a man went shooting up past him. In desperation, the man with the chute yelled, *"Hey do you know anything about parachutes?!"* The man flying past him looked down and yelled, *"No. Do you know anything about gas stoves?!"*

We need to carefully handle the information we get from Holy Spirit. At our church, we teach people that if they get a word, they should submit that word to those who are more seasoned before they give it. We also record any word which is spoken. If it's worth being spoken, it's worth being recorded and typed out to be remembered, studied, and understood. We encourage our people to share any prophecy they've received with someone they trust. The worst thing we can do is act on a spoken word before fully understanding what God's intentions are. Let's face it: people are not perfect. The word we receive may require some refinement from God Himself before we fully understand what He intended. In both the giving and receiving, personal prophecy must be handled carefully!

I knew a couple who was given a word that they were to go to Africa. They shared it with the church elders, and the elders had no witness of it—they could not agree with the couple's intentions. This couple wanted to sell everything they had and move to Africa. The elders disagreed but made the couple an offer: *"Close up your home, go to Africa, work there for 90 days. We'll help you. When you come back, if you feel that you are to return, we'll work with you to help you go back."*

Sounded like a great word to me. But the couple didn't think so. They got offended, left and went to another church. The elders at the new church heard about the couple's plans and gave them the same response. So the couple finally left that church, sold everything they owned, moved to a stable African nation and transferred all their money there. Three months later, the country fell into chaos and their long-term visas were denied. Without visas, they could not withdraw their money. They came back to the United States with nowhere to go, no money, nothing. It was a disaster.

There is safety in wise counsel. Submit and review a personal prophecy with those who have authority in your life. Everyone needs someone who has spiritual authority in their life. I thank God that I have 12 men in my life who will jerk my chain if I need it. (Sometimes I need it.) Being accountable to those who have spiritual authority in our lives is a safety net both for ourselves and for those dependent upon our lives.

In 1984, I had some visions about Australia. From these, I just knew I was going there that next year. Yet, for various reasons, it never came to be. But knowing me, I would have bought a ticket anyway and left! As it turned out, God held me in check. Eventually, I saw that it wasn't in His plan. The visions were something else which I did not understand at the time.

The Word of God comes with order, line upon line, precept upon precept, here a little, there a little. Exodus 23:30 says,

> *"Little by little I <God> will drive them <enemies> out from before you, until you have increased, and you inherit the land."*

Condemnation and Judgment

When the Lord speaks, it never brings condemnation. In Romans 8:1 it says,

> *"There is therefore now no condemnation to those who are in Christ Jesus, who do not walk according to the flesh, but according to the Spirit."*

God will never condemn us. I don't care what we did. I don't care how hard we have fallen. I don't care how many *times* we have fallen. He is not a condemner. He is a life-giver and He will not condemn us.

Equally important in the Christian life is the proper place for judgment. Now, it may seem to some readers that I have just contradicted myself. I just said that there is no condemnation and now I am extolling the virtues of judgment. The confusion comes from the fact that judgment is not condemnation. First of all, there are two types of judgment: righteous and unrighteous. Scripture tells us that a righteous man judges all things. Unrighteous judgment leads to condemnation. Condemnation starts with judgment and goes straight to sentencing and execution. Condemnation is passing sentence and then carrying it out.

Judgment brings conviction, which when we yield to it, leads to forgiveness, mercy and life. Condemnation is judgment without mercy and leads to death.

The common misunderstanding over Christians judging things comes from the scripture: *"Judge not, that you be not judged"* (Matthew 7:1). The word for "judge" in the Greek is actually the word "critique," as in critiquing a painting or a play. Jesus was really saying that we are criticized with the same measure with which we criticize others.

1 Peter 4:7 says:

"For the time has come for judgment to begin at the house of God."

God expects us to exercise mature judgment. Actually, Christians should judge all things. For example, if a prophetic word is given in my church, it is incumbent upon all who hear it to judge the word to determine the degree to which it comes from the heart of God. Without judgment, we would either accept everything that came out of a person or we would accept none of it.

The way to judge something is not on the basis of right or wrong, but on the basis of whether it brings life or death. We could argue for days whether it is right or wrong to drink alcohol, but if we can point to the manifestation of death in a person's life, we have the basis for saying, "You have a problem with alcohol and you need to give it up!"

Years ago, the Pentecostals moved into the former country of Zaire, Africa, as part of a missionary outreach. One of the first things they encountered was polygamy, and they struggled to address it doctrinally. On a simple right or wrong basis, polygamy was not allowed in the New Testament. But on a practical basis, divorcing all but one wife meant that the other wives and their children would become outcasts. Also, divorce was spoken of negatively in the Old Testament. The Pentecostal pastor at the time decided to instruct the men to keep their wives, as this would be best for all concerned, but that the young men of marrying age would be instructed to marry only once. However, this was not acceptable for the Pentecostal church; they eventually withdrew their support for this pastor and defrocked him. Yet the fruit of his early decision has vindicated him. Zaire (now the Democratic Republic of the Congo) is today 70% monogamous.

Without judgment, we are helplessly open to anything. 1 Corinthians 2:15 says, *"he who is spiritual judges all things...."* God wants the church to rise up and judge righteously. There is a difference between judging and carrying out the sentencing. We judge, God sentences.

I once pastored a great church. After the pioneering effort was done, I turned it over to one of my spiritual sons. Well, at the time, I thought he was a son. Within a year, the church was in turmoil with fighting, backbiting, confusion, and charges of financial mismanagement.

I paid a visit to the pastor soon after I heard about the troubles. After some initial discussion, I said to him: *"I've got three questions I want to ask you. First, who am I to you?"*

He said *"You are absolutely nothing to me, and as soon as I can get your smell out of this building, you'll be nothing to these people either."*

Well, I about fell out of my chair. The building he was holding church in was in my name and the mortgage was $400,000! I was the apostle over the entire operation. I wasn't trying to control it, but I expected some accountability from this man, especially since things were going so poorly. But none of this was received. He ended up leaving the church, taking some people with him and starting a store-front church in the same town.

One day as I was standing on the back deck of my house, thinking about all this, God spoke to me: *"If you'll judge that work, I'll deal with it."*

It took me several months before I could do what God said. Here's why: I knew that I could judge it and that God would deal with the situation. But I feared that God might eventually bless the man and then his church would grow bigger than mine. Now, I'm not proud of that, but I'm being honest. So it took a month of wrestling before I could judge this situation in the spirit. During that time, I consulted with my apostolic presbytery about the word I'd received, and they felt it was from God. So one Saturday night, as I was again on my back porch (I seem to do my best praying on my back porch while grilling) I looked toward heaven and said: *"Lord, I judge that work to be an Ishmael and I release it. Bless the man, do whatever you want with him."*

The following week, the man walked into his store-front church—he was running 50 or 60 at the time—and announced to the people: *"This work is an Ishmael. I started it to prove Clay Nash wrong. Now I'm closing it down."*

I judged the work, not the man. And I did not condemn either one. I didn't pass sentence and I didn't carry out a sentence. I left everything to God. God could have poured mercy into the situation and blessed that man mightily. The man could have had the biggest church in Tennessee after that day. But God chose to move in a different way, and to his credit, the man obeyed the word of God.

People-rule

God will always speak in line with His written Word. But isn't it amazing how sometimes we don't believe the written Word? How many of us know what "Laodicea" means? Most Christians think it means "lukewarm" because in the Book of Revelation, the Laodicean church was called a lukewarm church. But that's not what it means. The word 'Laodicea' means "people-rule." A church which is ruled by the people will become lukewarm towards God.

God establishes rule through the visionary, the "set-person," the person with the vision who has been "set" in place. When God establishes a congregation, He does so by first establishing the parameter.

Around the vision of the leader, He frames other people to complete the border. In the process, He establishes a common understanding, a sharing of vision, passion, and power to accomplish the work. From this framework, God fills in the rest of the congregation until the vision is complete.

Eternal

Matthew 24:35 says, *"Heaven and earth will pass away, but My words will by no means pass away."* When God speaks, He establishes things for eternity. There are words that God spoke thousands of years ago that are still powerful today. Everything that He established in the earth is still here. Every animal that has ever died on earth is still in the earth. It's simply in a different form. Every word that has ever been spoken by anyone who has ever lived in the earth is still here. Sound never stops; it changes frequency the further out it goes but it continues forever.

When God spoke to Adam and Eve, He blessed them and commissioned them, sending them forth in power which still propels mankind today. God did the same with Noah and his sons. He blessed them in the earth. The rainbow He established was actually the visual form of the sound of that blessing that went out over the earth. This may sound strange, but sounds have colors associated with them. I can't explain it, but I have seen this many times in the spirit.

Not only are our words eternal—much has been taught on this—but the intent of our words has a lasting impact. They create the spaces which we eventually inhabit. By speaking good words aligned with God and His will for our lives, we can create a good place to inhabit. Similarly, our negative words will create an unpleasant and evil space which we will eventually inherit.

Unfortunately, negativity seems to come more naturally to us. While we tend to see blessings as the result of God's exceptional favor, we tend to see difficulties, obstacles, and frustrations as normal for our lives. We accept these negative conditions as we do gravity, seeing God's blessings as a momentary uplift like a ride in a hot air balloon. When the air cools, we come back to "normal."

We need to step into a new paradigm. Our struggles and difficulties are not the norm; God's blessings ARE the norm. Our past lives in darkness have pre-set our perceptions; these need to change. We need to realign our lives for good.

Often our negative words escape our attention because they sound normal. Simple comments such as *"I knew the economy was going to fail,"* or *"It's just my luck,"* or *"Life's a struggle to test us,"* may seem harmless, even accurate. But inherent in these statements is a prevailing negative faith which takes root in us, spreads its branches and creates its own reality. When we acknowledge the economy's failure or our bad luck or our constant struggle, are we not also stating implicitly that we do not expect anything better? Of course we are. We are establishing our belief structure based on what we have experienced so far. This is how humans work; this is how life works. What we believe establishes who we are and structures our interaction with the world around us. Which is why Jesus stressed over and over: *"If you believe...."* He wants to change our belief system. He wants to change our faith.

When He speaks to us, it is from His paradigm—His frame of reference—His belief system—not ours. To understand His words, we must understand them from His paradigm as well.

The Word says that the tongue holds the power to life and death because words are the key to our existence. We have a new reality presented to us in the words of God. Our salvation means more than a rescue from the flames of hell. It also means we are rescued from a world system which keeps us trapped in bondage and separated from the fullness of God. The change from the world's reality to God's reality starts with words. *"In the beginning was the Word,..."* (John 1:1).

We have a difficult time with changing our words because it involves more than just reading the Bible. Faith comes by the God-breathed Word: the *Rhema* word. We can read the Bible until it runs out our ears and down our back, but until we make a God-connection, the word remains *logos* and not *rhema*. Secular scholars spend their lives studying the Bible and never experience the touch of God. This is because they are not seeking God; they are seeking scholastic achievement or perhaps a cure for insomnia.

Our words are eternal; our lives are eternal. Let's make them God's.

Believing God's Voice

Susan and I once tried to buy a building for a church we were establishing. I made an offer which involved financing, and the owner said, *"Pastor Nash, I've got a cash-offer from some other folks which I'm going to take because I don't want to finance it."* I got off that phone feeling shattered; my faith was shaken. The Sunday before, God had told me that the building was mine, and I'd announced it to the congregation. We were meeting in a temporary facility at the time and were looking forward to having our own building.

I was racked with doubts—not doubts about God, but of myself. Did I hear the Lord clearly? Did I act in haste? Should I have kept quiet until we had secured the building? What do I tell the church now?

I finally decided that I had heard God clearly, so I made an announcement that Sunday that we need to put our faith into action. I gathered some church members and we made a trek to the building to conduct a Jericho march around it. We looked through the building windows, reminding ourselves of what God spoke to us. We told everybody we saw that this was our building. At one point, pride rose up in me and I thought, *"I'm going to look like a fool if all of this falls through. I'm really out on a limb now."* But all of a sudden, faith rose up in me and I said, *"No! I heard God speak, and this building is ours!"* I spoke into the heavens and said, *"It's good someone else is buying the building, because they're buying it to give it to me! It's my building; God said it's my building. They aren't getting my building! They can't have it. It's mine! Thank you, Lord, it's mine!"*

That was on a Monday. On Thursday the owner called me and said, *"Pastor Nash, the people buying that building backed out. I'm accepting your deal."* Praise God! As of this writing, we still own that building and God is being served there. When God speaks, we KNOW we've heard His voice! Faith rises in us. Regardless of what's going on—we might waiver for just a moment like I did—if we will go back to what God said, then faith will bring us through to the other side!

Iron Sharpens Iron

When God speaks, His word is precise, direct, and sharp enough to penetrate anything in its way to accomplishing the purpose for which it was sent. As a prophet, I've learned that the three most heart-penetrating words I can speak are: *"Jesus loves you."*

In 1984, I led 48 truck drivers to the Lord. It was incredible to watch God move in those truck stops and restaurants. Now, truck drivers are known to be a blunt, burly bunch with big egos and even bigger chips on their shoulders. I know what I'm talking about; I owned a trucking company and was raised in the industry. I grew up among these people, and when I grew in Christ, I developed a burden for them. I'd hang out in truck stops, looking for an opportunity to give them a word of knowledge or perhaps pray with them if they'd let me. I didn't care how hard they seemed on the outside. The most powerful thing I could share with them was, *"Hey, Jesus loves you. You know that?"* And these men (they were mostly men, but there were a few women as well) would drop to their knees right in the truck stop and get right with God. God's word, sharper than any sword, pierced them right between the wheat and the chaff. They were not the same when they got up off the floor. For one thing, their coffee was colder, but for another, their hearts were on fire. Psalms 119:89 says, *"Forever, O LORD, Your word is settled in heaven."*

Love

Of course, the all-pervading characteristic of the voice of God is love. Everything He says and does regarding our lives is based on His loving nature. He is love; one hundred percent. It is His underlying motive in all things. Even when He's being harsh, the root of His motivation is still love.

I remember my parents telling me during times of discipline,

"Son, this is going to hurt us worse than it hurts you." I thought my Dad was insane when he'd say that. But then I got kids of my own and I understood what he meant. It does hurt to chastise a loved-one. Discipline would be easier in the short run if love was not part of the relationship. But God's discipline is based on love. From my experience, I've actually been angriest with my children when I see them hurting someone I dearly love: themselves! The correction I administered during those times was to restore them to the place where they could receive God's love for themselves.

Love is unmistakable in the voice of God; His voice is filled with love, overflowing with love, nothing but love.

Chapter 7

Fundamentals of Prophecy

When I was a boy, my dad gave me a pedal-powered John Deere riding tractor. It was metal—everything was metal in those days. The dinosaurs had just passed into extinction and plastic was yet to be invented. I loved to ride my tractor, pumping the pedals, turning the wheel, and pretending I was a real farmer. I was also driven mad, wondering how the thing worked: how pumping the pedals made the rear wheels spin, how the steering wheel made the front wheels turn, and what made it stop.

So one day, I got my dad's hammer and beat my tractor to pieces to see what was inside it. Oddly, it never worked after that, but I did learn something about mechanics. I also learned something about myself: I'm a mechanical type of person, especially with a hammer in my hand, and I will tear anything apart to learn about it.

Perhaps that is why people are always surprised when I talk about the fundamentals of prophecy. "Isn't it just out there," they say. "In the ether? A will-o'-the-wisp? A figment of God's imagination?"

Well, no it's not. Prophecy is substantive. It is actually governed by firm rules—metaphysics, if you will—some of which we derive from experience and others we develop from a study of the Bible. There are some aspects to prophecy which I won't be able to explain but I do know they work. Other aspects, I can point straight to the word for explanation.

When I say that prophecy is substantive, I like to give the following example. Anyone familiar with the things of the spirit knows that spiritual things have a reality all their own. As I said, spiritual things are not wispy, phantom-like things. They have substance, they have body, they have dimensions and clear parameters. In fact, the realness of spiritual things exceeds the realness of what most of us consider the "real" world.

I was in Zaire, Africa, preaching a series of meetings to a large crowd. At the end of my speaking, I gave an altar call for anyone to come forward for prayer to receive the Baptism of the Holy Spirit. Now, where I come from in the United States, I would get about 10 people out of a large crowd who would respond. But that night in Africa, a thousand people stood up and rushed forward. Overwhelmed and panicking, I cried, *"Lord, what do I do now?"* He said, *"Just pray for them all at once."* So that's what I did—one mass prayer for a thousand people to receive the baptism of the Holy Spirit. And as they each received the Holy Spirit, it literally sounded like a thunderous waterfall growing in power. I'll never forget that. Substance was pouring out over those people, something more real than the waters of Niagara. And it rocked the place!

Manifestation vs. Gift

But what exactly is prophecy?

> *"...there are diversities of charismas < graces> but it is the same Spirit."*

This tells us that all believers share the same Spirit. Reading further:

> *"There are diversities of ministries, and there are diversities of activities but the manifestation of the Spirit is given to each one for the profit of all."* (1 Cor. 12: 4-7)

The instruction in 1 Corinthians calls prophecy a manifestation of Holy Spirit. Recall that 1 Cor. 12:1 instructs us to discern "the spiritual," not "the spiritual gifts." Prophecy is not a gift. Rather, it is a manifestation of spiritual substance. In 1 Cor. 12:10, it says,

> *"and to another miracles, to another prophecy, to another discerning of spirits, to another diverse kinds of tongues, to another interpretation of tongues."*

The Greek word for prophecy is *prohetia*. It actually means a discourse emanating from a divine inspiration with the purposes of God. Prophecy is inspirational.

God has given His Holy Spirit, and Holy Spirit gives manifestations of Himself. Now tradition teaches that there are nine gifts of Holy Spirit. I do not like the term "gifts" because it takes away from the fundamental understanding that these are really nine manifestations of the same Holy Spirit which we all share. Too many people get caught up in the idea that they have "this gift," or "that gift." Then I hear: *"Sorry, I don't have that gift, I only have this one."* In fact, we all have Holy Spirit. We have access to all His manifestations.

While we emphasize understanding of who we are and what our place is in the Body of Christ, we can miss the greater point. Yes, it's great to feel good about ourselves, to finally have answers to our natures which have plagued us since our days in darkness, but as the Spirit said to me early in my ministry: *"If you're only seeking to discover your spiritual gifting to benefit you, then you will never discover it."* Certainly, there are personal benefits to discovering, developing, and operating in our gifts, but we only experience these benefits when we recognize that the true reason for the gifts is to minister God to other people.

To re-emphasize, 1 Corinthians says: *"the manifestation is given to each one for the profit of all"* (1 Cor. 12:7). He manifests the one for the profit of all.

When Heaven and earth come into agreement thru the declaration of an obedient child of God, the prophetic manifests. When prophecy manifests in a gathering of believers, it causes four things to happen:

1. People's heart-secrets are revealed.

2. People are brought into the presence of God.

3. People worship God.

4. Unbelievers know that God is present.

As we see from this list, the benefits of the prophetic manifestation are not restricted to the person receiving the prophecy. While the message may be focused on a specific individual or group, the effects of the prophecy emanate from the prophet like shock waves from the epicenter of an earthquake, profiting every person with the manifest presence of God.

There is a modern theology which says that there is no such thing as a word of prophecy today. Instead, prophecy is defined as inspired preaching or teaching. While I consider myself a prophetic preacher, I don't believe that this is the extent of the spiritual manifestation called prophecy—obviously! Inspired preaching has a prophetic tone to it, but God also speaks prophetically into people's lives today just as He has since He created Adam.

Adding to the misunderstanding is the fact that the prophetic is not always flashy. It doesn't grab headlines like miracles do. And when prophecy is brought to the forefront of public consciousness, it is not always presented in the best light. When a seven-month pregnant woman hauls someone bodily from a burning car, it makes headlines as an act of faith resulting in superhuman energy. However, when a prophet stands up and says that a city needs to repent before calamity strikes, the public writes the prophet off as a misguided nut. In movies, prophets are portrayed as crazy-eyed old men with long, unkempt beards, wandering aimlessly about city streets, crying out unintelligible words and ranting about the Harleys they once owned.

Substance

Prophecy is the discourse emanating from the divine inspiration, declaring the word of God either by reproving and admonishing the wicked, or by comforting the afflicted. It is hidden words revealed, especially those foretelling future events.

Prophecy operates on several different levels. Motivationally, it deals with correction, encouragement, admonishment, warning, and insight. Positionally, it deals with the present, the past, and/or the future.

As I said earlier, prophecy—like all spiritual things—is more than just words. It has substance. The substance of prophecy is made up of three components:

1. Words of knowledge — past?

2. Words of wisdom — future

3. Love

Words of knowledge contain information from God which bring understanding of our past into our present reality. Words of knowledge are never about the future. We can only have knowledge about those things that have already occurred. Hence, words of knowledge are forth-telling: they reveal the past.

For example, I might say to a friend: *"Pastor, I saw a vision of you driving through a real sharp curve, and there was a wreck ahead, but I saw that you weren't hurt. God protected you."* Now, that was a word of knowledge because it pertained to an event in the past.

Words of wisdom, on the other hand, speak to our present reality about the future. They have a foretelling (as opposed to a forth-telling) perspective. Following the same example, I might say to a friend: *"Pastor, on your way home today, there is going to be a wreck on Elbow Road. Take another way home to avoid it."*

Between knowledge and wisdom is the crucial substantive element to prophecy: love. By the measure of love, we are able to judge the spirit in which a prophecy is given. Contrary to common thought, spiritual power, authority, and insight are not the markers of true, Godly prophecy. Many spirits have power and authority, and any being can lie cleverly about the past, present, or future. Godly prophecy, however, is saturated with God's love. Its motivation is love, its direction—even in correction—conveys love, and the final fruit is love. Prophecy which is not given in the spirit of love (read: Holy Spirit) is known to be not from God. Prophecy without love is false prophecy.

To illustrate my point, note that in 1 Corinthians, chapter 12 addresses manifestations involving knowledge, and chapter 14 addresses manifestations involving wisdom. Sandwiched in between these two is chapter 13, which addresses love.

When I began my ministry as a prophet of God, I didn't have the wisdom, tenderness or brokenness that I needed to adequately convey God's love. I had the word of the Lord but I handled it in a way that hurt people more than helped them. Twenty-plus years later, I have evolved. Yes, truth is truth. But truth will only prevail if it's presented correctly. It must be accepted by the recipient before it can prevail in their lives. What if Jesus had taken to kicking people in the shins before telling them that God loved them? Seems ridiculous, doesn't it? But how different is it when we say *"Hear the word of the Lord..."* and then deliver prophetic words with an attitude which says, *"I could care less if you lived or died."* When we speak God's words into people's lives, we are doing more than uttering divine words. We are—for that brief moment—representing God to them in all His manifestations:

God who *loves.*

God who *avenges.*

God who *knows.*

God who *wonders.*

God who *comforts.*

God who *challenges.*

God who *cajoles.*

God who *answers.*

God who *questions.*

God who *seeks.*

God who *leads.*

A young man named Tony used to come to our church for a few weeks each year. We would minister to him, then he'd go back into the world and resume his sinful lifestyle until the next time we saw him. Finally, he came and received deliverance and counseling for his homosexual lifestyle. During that particular time of ministry, which was conducted in the midst of the congregation, the word of

Lord came to me, and I told him straight out: *"Tony, if you go back into that lifestyle, you'll catch a disease and die."* It was a stern word, and it actually offended some people, so much so that they left the church over it. They said they could not be part of a church where the pastor spoke to people in that fashion. Interestingly, the person who was the least offended was Tony himself. He heeded that word, got healed, and stayed out of his sinful lifestyle. He told me some time later that the thing which reached him the most was not the word I spoke, but the tears running down my face. See, that word—stern as it was—was delivered in love. Tony told me that the people who left the church over that word were fools. Those aren't my words, they're his. But I can't say I disagree.

Prophetic words are the thrust of God's spiritual substance into our verbally attuned universe. The heart of the prophet must reflect Jesus' love. Knowing truth is one thing; properly handling truth is all together different.

King Solomon had two women brought before him with a peculiar story. Now, to my reckoning, these two women didn't just walk up to the King and say, *"We need to meet with you."* Instead, they probably arranged an appointment through the king's intermediaries. I suspect that one of Solomon's aides said to him, *"There's two women claiming to be the mother of the same child. They will be here next Thursday at 11:00."*

And Solomon said, *"Oh no! Two feuding women! Can't I go fight the Philistines instead?"*

No, he probably didn't say that. But I do believe that the wise King would have sent out some aides to get to the bottom of the matter: canvass the neighborhood where they lived, talk to relatives, gather intelligence, get at the truth before the moment of truth arrived.

Armed with this information, on the day they came before Solomon, he could boldly say, *"OK, you claim the child, and you claim child. Great! We'll cut him in half and call it even!"* Solomon knew full well that the true mother would say, *"No, she can have him."*

Here is the key: I believe Solomon already knew (or strongly suspected) who the real mother was, but he took that truth and presented it in a wise manner so that truth would prevail. Had he simply given the child to the correct mother, as determined by his investigation, the false mother would have cried out that she had been defrauded. But as it went, the false mother was convicted by her own words. Who but the charlatan would have assented to the butchering of this baby boy? And now the whole court knew who the imposter was as well.

When we combine words of wisdom, words of knowledge, and God's love, we get prophecy. Prophecy always deals with the past and the future together, bound by love. If someone gives a word which only touches on one of these, then it is really a Word of Knowledge or Word of Wisdom, or maybe just some encouraging advice. It is not prophecy.

As great as it sounds, prophecy can be abused. People get lazy, and rather than seeking a word from God on their own, they rely on someone with a prophetic emphasis to lead them. This will lead to sickness, weakness, and error. I've been a prophet of God for many years, and I have words for certain people within me, but God won't release me to give them because the individuals are not ready. They don't want to hear from God; they simply want a word from a prophet to make them feel better for a while. God doesn't work that way.

A few years ago, I was at an annual prophetic conference. I'd been there the year before to speak, and when I went back the next year, I saw many of the same people sitting in the same places, at the same level of growth as they were last year. As I pondered this, the Lord spoke to me: *"They are back to get another word, and they haven't done anything with the word they got last year."*

Please note the phrase God used: *"they haven't done anything..."* The prophetic word of the Lord is not a trophy that we put on the shelf. It is not a warm bottle with a rubber nipple to comfort us. Paul told Timothy to wage the good warfare over the words of prophecy that had been spoken into his life. (See I Timothy 1:18.) In other words: FIGHT FOR THEM! Declare them in the face of the enemy. Believe them and never let go of them. Stand on them as a bridge to the living God!

I am conscious of this in my own life. Since I travel in many prophetic circles, I have received many prophetic words. Three times a year I get those words out and read every one of them to the devil, saying: *"Ha, ha, here is what God said about this and that!"* If we believe that God speaks prophetically, then we need to handle these words carefully and honor them in our lives, using them for our growth as God intended.

Motivations for Prophecy

A prophetic anointing can be "pulled" upon. Because of this, prophets need to understand that not every unction to give a word is straight from God. Sometimes it is the people around the prophet, pulling on the prophet's anointing, who create the "need" to prophesy. Sometimes it is the prophets themselves who think they need to prophesy. We need discernment in this area for the body of Christ to remain healthy.

I was at a conference led by an internationally-known prophet. There were two teenaged members of the worship team who carried an awesome presence of God, so the other prophet and I began to prophesy to these young men. Now, I've done many conferences around the world with this man, and we have prophesied the paint off the walls. I trust his integrity, as he does mine. At this conference, as we finished up ministering to these two young men, there appeared eight more people around us who began to prophesy to the same young men.

The conference leader leaned over to me and asked, *"What's going on?"*

"What do you mean?"

"Something's not right about this."

I thought for a moment and said: *"Those people are prophesying because they need to prophesy, not because of the words they are prophesying."*

Everything the eight people spoke that day lined up with the word of God, but their motivation was rooted in a need to be seen and affirmed for doing something prophetic.

Knowing this tendency, I continually and ruthlessly examine my own motives for ministry. Why do I want to minister? What do I expect to get from it? Have I really any words to give? Am I really trying to serve God and help others, or am I merely trying to meet my own needs? I live my life with a proverbial sticker above my forehead which reads: UNDER CONSTRUCTION.

If we want to understand our motivations, we must look at our passions. What is it that we really want? What engages us thoroughly? What drives us to the point where we forget all else, sell out, and obtain the single pearl? Our passions lead us to our motivations. But to find these, we have to be honest with ourselves and our Creator.

I lay my life out before God, knowing that His love is enough to cover me. I do not fear condemnation from Him. I have learned that I am loved as I am, and this causes me to open, to change, to be more as He created me to be. I can submit to God because I know He loves me unabashedly, without reservation. He waits patiently for me to say, *"Hey God, something's not quite right about this thing in me. Let's get it right."* Then He corrects it.

Sometimes people come to my church saying that they have a word. After examining it, I may ask them to hold it until the timing is right. See, we can have the word of the Lord, even have the right motivation, but we must also have the right timing. A word spoken out of God's timing will fall fruitless to the ground.

I learned much of this the hard way. I used to own a trucking company. Towards the end of my business days, as I was moving into ministry, I picked up a load of strawberries in California and brought them to Lafayette, LA.

We had just planted a church in Arkansas, and I was going to service that night. However, I was not the senior minister. I had prayed all that day in the Spirit—I used to pray 16 hours a day as I drove my rig across the interstate—and the Lord spoke to me as I drove. When I came home, I went into church during the worship. When there was a time to prophesy, I stood up and gave the word that God gave me. It was a powerful word, but it went over like a bowling ball tossed in a gutter. It did not fly.

Later, I went to my pastor and said, *"Pastor Don, I repent. I didn't know, please forgive me. I'm sorry I stood up and gave that word. I don't understand. I prayed all day in tongues and God showed me this vision and told me that this was a word for this church and I just knew it was God and I'm sorry. I give you my word: I will never prophesy again."*

But he was a wise pastor and he said, *"No, you will prophesy again, and you'll learn to do it right. It is your calling."*

So at the beginning of my work week, I hauled a load of shower doors to L.A., got some more strawberries, came back to Lafayette, LA, and on Sunday morning during worship, I felt the anointing come. This time, I said, *"Nope, God, I ain't doing this again."* But God kept dealing with me and I finally broke down and gave the word. It was the same word, no different from the one I'd given the week before, but this time it flew like an eagle. I mean: it left a white spot on the floor and feathers twirling in the air as it took off! It was right on! The timing meant everything.

I said at the beginning of this chapter that I am very mechanical. Here is an example that the gear-head readers can relate to.

Every mechanic knows that General Motors developed the small-block Chevy engine. It is a very durable, spunky V8 engine with a unique characteristic. It is possible to put it on two different firing orders. (Firing order is the order in which the spark plugs fire into the cylinders.) The normal firing order can be changed to a second order, such that the motor will still start and idle smoothly. To all appearances, it is in perfect order. But if the driver tries to pull away, the engine will stall and die. It simply has no power in this timing order. (This is fun to do to a friend's truck.)

Just as in small-block Chevys, proper timing in prophecy is everything. What seems perfect at idle, gathering energy on the tarmac and ready to take off, can utterly fail when put to real use. This was the school that God was carrying me through as I delivered strawberries. *All things work together for good to those who love God, to those who are the called according to His purpose* (Romans 8:28). I needed to make those mistakes so I could be taught. And the strawberries tasted pretty good, too.

Accountability

The prophetic anointing brings a greater level of accountability, both to the prophet and to the one receiving the prophecy. For this reason, it has to be taken very seriously. We must prove every prophetic word with Biblical principles, by Holy Spirit, and with the witness of those in authority over our lives. No word from God will ever violate Biblical principles. Which is not to say that it won't violate our present doctrine. That is a completely different matter. However, before the prophecy is acted upon, it should be clearly understood biblically, with the theological issues worked through and the backing of our spiritual partners obtained.

I used to meet every week with an apostolic leader in Memphis. I was submitted to him as an apostle in my life. Months earlier, I had received a word to plant a church in a town located between where I was pastoring and where he pastored. I was just waiting on the timing to begin this church. On a Monday, as I was driving into Memphis to meet this leader, the Lord said, *"It's time to plant this church."* Now, nothing excites me more than church planting. This is what I live for! And as I drove on, I grew more excited. I met with my apostle and shared with him what God had said, and he looked across his desk at me and said, *"No, I don't witness that. I believe you are nine months to a year premature, and I won't bless this now."* I was crushed!

Well, I am a man who hears God, and I knew I had heard God through this man, even if it did crush me. I finally got home late that night and prayed, *"Hey, God, in the morning, I need to talk to you."* See, I figured He was busy that night with everybody else's problems, and I wanted to make sure I had His full attention. So I got up the next morning at 4 am and said, *"Lord, I know I heard your voice telling me it's time to plant that church, but when I submitted it to the man of God, he said I was premature and that he wouldn't bless it."*

God said, *"Did I ask you to submit your life and ministry to his authority?"*

I said, *"Yes, Lord."*

Then I waited for Him to give me a 20 minute discourse on everything I needed to know. But He said nothing!

After spending sometime before the Lord, I began to understand that these two different words from God did not nullify each other, even though they were contradictory. God had told me to submit myself to this man's authority, and that had not changed, even though the man did not approve of the church plant at this time. I submitted to the first word (through the apostle) and watched God mature me through my obedience.

Well, 45 days later, the apostle called me and said, *"Clay, I don't know what shifted but it's time to plant that church. When you get ready to go, I'll commit support each month to the church plant."*

See, I could have just stepped out from under that man's authority, but I would have been stepping out from under God's authority, because it was God who told me to submit to that man in the first place. And in the process, I learned how to work with contradictory versions of God's voice.

Conditional vs. Non-Conditional Prophecy

Most prophecy is conditional upon a proper biblical response, though not all prophecy appears to be conditional. Now, some prophecy is obviously conditional, as when the prophet says: *"If you will go to Atlanta and start a church, then I will bless that work."* Other conditional prophecy is not so obvious, such as when we hear: *"God is calling you to become a doctor for the poor overseas."* What's not so obvious is that the person receiving this word still must get accepted to medical school, pass the courses, apply for a missionary position, and actually *become* that doctor. All with God's blessing, of course.

Oddly, these preconditions would be very obvious to a non-Christian. If I told a non-Christian that they should become a doctor and work with the poor, and if they heeded my advice, they would make plans to enter school, pass the course of study, and then work with some charitable agency.

The Christian, on the other hand, might be expecting God to do it all. I mean, we serve a mighty god, do we not? A God who can do all that we can exceedingly ask or think, right? Sure we do. And God said He was calling us to become a doctor and sending us to the mission field. Well, have at it, God! Make me a doctor! And I'll sit right here—in faith—until You do!

People tend to hear what they want to hear. Which is why, as a prophet, we must be accurate in giving the exact message God gives to us for a person. God knows who He is talking to; the prophet does not always know. If a person is lazy, then hearing that God is going to do such and such can give license to their passive lifestyle. On the other hand, a word which says, *"Arise, go, and do!"* will have a much different effect on a person. They either get up and go or they don't.

While most prophecy is conditional, some prophecy is unconditional. God says it and it happens. Period. Katie bar the door. Too wet to plow. End of story.

An example of unconditional prophecy is when Peter spoke to Ananias and Sapphire. Peter prophetically revealed their sin, uttered God's judgment, and waited for their dead, warm bodies to hit the floor. Nothing conditional about that.

A man in Dyersburg, TN, once came to me and asked that I pray about whether he should buy a certain building for his church. I knew this man well. I'd helped him plant this church—he was a great pastor—and he was seeking to grow his church. Well, I prayed and the Lord told me that the man shouldn't buy the building. God said that instead of purchasing the building the pastor had in mind, there was a building that would be given to the pastor. I thought this was a great word, but when I shared it with the pastor, he grew angry with me and began to separate from me in relationship and accountability.

I went on praying for the man and blessing him, endeavoring to be his friend, but I wasn't getting very far. Finally, the Lord told me to tell him that if he bought that building, he would die prematurely. I can tell you, that is a grievous word to share with anybody. But in obedience, I humbly shared the word with the pastor. He grew angrier. About 16 months later, after purchasing the building and severing all ties with me, the bank had foreclosed on him, took the building back, and he died of complications from diabetes, quite possibly brought on by stress. It broke my heart. He was a great man of God who would not heed an unconditional word from God.

We can only speak prophetically into a person's life to the degree that we have relationship with them. There is a reason that Jesus spent three years living with the men who would carry on the work of the church after He ascended. Jesus was able to speak things into those men's lives based on relationship with them. This even continued after He left the earth. In the case of this pastor, I worked hard on the relationship so that he would receive the word God gave me for him. In the end, he rejected relationship with me because he did not want the word I brought. I'm not sure why he rejected the word; possibly out of distrust of me and my motives rather than outright rebellion against God. I doubt this pastor realized he was setting himself up against God. I suspect he knows it now.

Certainly, we can approach a total stranger and share things which they will receive, but this is a rare occurrence which God prepares them for. Even so, such encounters require that the person accept us in that moment. If they think us a fraud, or a lunatic, or even a misguided religious zealot, they will turn us off and reject what we are saying. The source has to be credible in order for the word to be received. God works through relationship, even in the prophetic.

The Bible tells us the traditions of men make the word of God of no effect. Traditions are built on the will of man, which is a powerful force to overcome when there is no trust. When we trust God in certain areas, we allow Him to lead us in those areas. Change comes as our trust grows.

As a prophet, I am trusted where I am known. The people around me know me. When I give a word, they trust me enough to receive the word and respond to it as God leads. I do <u>NOT</u> expect people to act on a prophecy simply because I speak it. That would be a cult. I lead and direct people as a servant of God. We are both accountable to the same Lord.

In 1986, I shared a word with a business man in Arkansas that on the 23rd of March, he would come into $579,000 dollars, but that if he did not do what God was going to tell him to do, then by the 30th of April, he would be filing bankruptcy. That's a pretty short period of time to go through that much money. Which is why, I suspect, that he didn't believe me at the time.

On the 23rd day of March, he came into the money. God told him to bless a small, rural church in Brinkley, Arkansas, with $30,000. He didn't do it. By April 30th, he was filing for re-organizational bankruptcy. It took him 10 years to get his financial house back in order. For years afterwards, every time he'd see me, he would say, *"Man, if you ever get another word for me, please give it and I'll obey it."* In retrospect, the word from God which this man disobeyed was given to help him AVOID bankruptcy, but he ran from that word like a child fleeing a frantic parent while chasing a ball into the street.

The Lord once told me to bless a pastor who was starting a Christian radio station. I pledged $1,200 dollars. Later I found out that he had reached out in an unrighteous way to a businessman in another pastor's church. He got the businessman to give him $60,000 dollars. The way he went about this was unethical and it made me angry, so I didn't pay the rest of the pledge.

Later that fall we found ourselves in a financial famine. I told the elders in my church that something was wrong. I recalled the scripture in Eccl. 10:8, where it says, *"If you break the hedge, the serpent will bite you."* When I find myself going through hard times, I first look at myself for the reason. I don't blame the devil. I don't blame other people. I don't blame the church or the government. Get this: I don't even blame my spouse! A long time ago, I met my enemy and I know him well. I see him every morning when I shave (and no, growing a beard does not help). I have more problems wrestling with myself than I do wrestling with any other opponent.

I went away for a few days, locked myself up in prayer, and the Lord revealed to me that I had not completed that pledge to the pastor with the radio station. Now, at that particular time, the church didn't have the money. I mean, we were down to rock bottom and I was running a credit line through my personal checking account. But I obeyed, paid the remainder of my pledge, and four weeks later we took up a first-fruits offering in a church of about 125. Bless God, $70,000 came in. I don't believe that much would have come in if I hadn't sought God and obeyed.

The Bible says it is better not to make a vow than to make one and not keep it. In Lev. 5:4 it says,

> *"If a man makes a vow, even an unsolicited one, that when he's reminded of it, he is to keep it."*

As important as it is to fulfill our vows, we can also be released from a vow. And at times, we should release others. I once had a man make a $100,000 vow to me. He only paid me $5,000 and then he lost three multi-million dollar businesses. His finances were in shambles. When I heard about this, I tired to contact him to release him from his vow, but he would not take my call. Finally, I spoke into the heavens and said, *"Lord, I release that man from his vow to me."* I did not want him to go broke. I didn't want him to lose those businesses. I wasn't going to ask him for the money. I just wanted to talk to him and release him from his vow.

Remember: prophecy has substance, it has mechanics, and it has accountability. It is more than just a gentle breeze. It is like the airstream which can carry a Boeing 777. In this case, it carries the church.

Chapter 8

Activating the Prophetic

"Most assuredly, I say to you, he who believes in Me, the works that I do he will do also; and greater works than these he will do, because I go to My Father. (John 14:12)

There is so much more to the prophetic, we have only touched the surface. However, I did not write this book simply to display my own works and talents. Nor did I write it only as a testimony to God's hand in my life. I wrote this book to activate the prophetic in you, dear reader. While I have poured out my heart in these pages in an attempt to give a taste of my 25 years living with the prophetic anointing, the ultimate payoff is for you to begin experiencing it yourself.

In the process, I have sought to take the prophetic out of the realm of the murky mystical and into the realm of the practical. If we are anything in relationship to God, we are called to be comfortable with the mystical on an everyday basis. We must welcome the common occurrence of God's presence, His favor, His communion. When we position ourselves to hear Him, we become prophetic.

In ministry, I use a series of exercises designed to acquaint people with the prophetic anointing while removing fears of the unknown and failure. These are simple exercises, deliberately crafted as a safe introduction to the prophetic.

I stress "safe" because, let's face it, the phrase, "Thus sayeth the Lord," is a powerful phrase, assuming of course that it is indeed "the Lord" who "thus sayeth." God help the man or woman who utters such a phrase unknowingly or worse, manipulatively. If we think that prophetic phrases and inflections add authority to our words, we are right. That is how people were created. We naturally respond to our Creator or to anything which sounds like our Creator. However, we must recognize that God takes His word seriously, and the accountability on the prophetic anointing is severe.

Am I trying to scare you? Yes and no. I want you to realize what you are about to enter into, and I want you to appreciate the power—both God's power and human power—which is released as we move into the prophetic realm.

It is difficult to complete a prophetic activation from the pages of a book. The exercises I discuss in this chapter need to be worked with those in ministry around you—preferably your local church. Normally when I take people through these activation exercises, I surround them with a ministry team of my choosing or a group of their peers (again, from their local church, if possible). This is effective for several reasons.

Most importantly, a team is necessary to move beyond unity and into a realm of oneness. Scripture is clear; that *we know in part and we prophesy in part* (I Corinthians 13:9). To get the complete picture, it takes all of us (or as many as are available) working in the spirit of oneness. Jesus taught that *"where two or three are gathered together in My name, I am there in the midst of them"* (Matthew 18:20). Which is why I do prophetic retreats with a team beside me. We get the totality of Jesus' ministry and the completeness of His anointing when people are joined in His name. We also stay out of trouble.

You see, we need accountability. Just as speaking in God's name is both powerful and subject to misuse, likewise when a person puts themselves under the anointing of another—as in student to teacher—a powerful bond occurs, facilitating spiritual impartation. This is fine, as long as everything is right in God. The danger comes when things are not. Think of a patient laying on an operating table, guts flayed open, vital organs being dissected by a surgeon. As long as the doctor is qualified, properly motivated, and surrounded by a skilled team, all will be well. This is no place for "Whoops!" "Oops."

I want people under my ministry to understand that being placed in a body of believers is necessary to avoid deception and error. As we step out into new spiritual realms, we are going to make mistakes. The more experienced and seasoned among us (read: old!) are best equipped to help us such that a minor fall leads us to a major lift.

It burdens me that people do not experience the prophetic realm on a regular basis. Ignorance and abuse of power are two reasons why they do not. My prayer is that you learn to walk hand in hand with the God who longs to commune with His people and activate His prophets.

Now, LET'S GET GOING!

Basis for Activation

The key to activating the prophetic in Christians is understood from Jesus' teaching on binding and loosening. When Jesus gave Christians the keys to the kingdom, He said:

> *"Whatever you bind on earth will be bound in heaven, and whatever you loose on earth will be loosed in heaven." (Matthew 16:19)*

Sounds simple, right? We have the right to bind, and we have the right to loose. However, we have to bind and loose the correct things. The clues for how to do this are uncovered when we understand what the scripture actually says in the original text:

> *"Whatever you bind (declare to be improper and unlawful) on earth must be <u>what is already bound</u> in heaven; and whatever you loose (declare lawful) on earth must be <u>what is already loosed</u> in heaven" (Matthew 16:19, Amp, underline added).*

Hopefully this makes a bit more sense. What we manifest on Earth is what has already been established in Heaven. For example, scripture tells us that God has bound all sickness in heaven. Can we agree that there is no sickness in heaven? Because of that truth, we have the right to bind sickness here on earth. Nothing will manifest itself on earth until it has been established in heaven, decreed on earth, released out of heaven, and received on earth.

In the spiritual realm, there are those called to walk in the prophetic and there are those called to be actual prophets. However, none of this can happen until that which is in heaven is called forth on earth. This is why, in my ministry, I call forth the prophets of

God to take their rightful place on earth: interspersed among the kingdoms of man. I call prophets into the church. I call prophets into business, into government, into finance, into the arts, into entertainment. I loose the call of God in people's lives. I call all of this into being in Jesus' name.

Yet as dramatic as this sounds—and I mean every word of it—the start of prophetic activation often involves baby steps. It is a process of turning, adjusting, and fine tuning.

I love the word tuning (though I am showing my age). When I was knee-high to a toadstool, radios were still analog. They had tuning knobs (frequency oscillators) to dial in a desired station. When the receiving signal became weak, it would drift off frequency and the sound would grow weak and distorted. Of course, in the 60's, we didn't care if our music was distorted. But for mellower music, we would grab the tuning knob and tweak it back to the correct frequency. Once the radio was tuned, we would again be able to hear the radio station clearly again.

I am helping you fine-tune yourself into recognizing the voice of God.

First Exercise

Allow me to introduce a few activation exercises designed to fine-tune your ability to recognize the voice of God and teach you how to release it into the earth, often into the lives of others. As a start, please get a sheet of paper and simply write:

My child, I love you very much and I want you to know...

Then become very quiet and listen intently with your heart, meditating on God's love for you and allowing Him to speak to you. Let His word come simply at first. If you are expecting clear words and phrases, you may be disappointed. As we discussed earlier, God often speaks through impressions, images, feelings, even smells. He also speaks through scripture, bringing to mind verses we might know or not know. By opening your heart and putting your mind in proper mode, you can make yourself available to recognize the voice of God.

This exercise is designed to put you in a frame of mind where you are dwelling on God's love. The reality of God's love is a powerful truth that dispels doubt—the great devourer of faith: the key element in our relationship with God. Anyone who enters into relationship with God must soon come to the realization of His deep and abiding love. All communication and spiritual impartation from Him is rooted in this simple fact: He loves us. Let Him speak to you now through that bond of love.

In preparation for this, you might also enhance your focus on spiritual things by putting on some soft music, taking time to set aside concerns and issues in your heart, and remove any distractions. Turn off your cell phone, quiet your soul, and lock your kids in a closet.

OK, just kidding on that last one. I am not endorsing locking kids in a closet. They'll get out and call Social Services. Better to bribe them. A few dollars, a bowl of popcorn each, and a wholesome DVD usually buys an hour's peace.

During this time, do not be afraid to write whatever comes to your heart and mind. By taking the risk and writing what you feel is coming to you, it will open you up to move into a realm of expectancy that can become a new way of living. You might simply sense a Scripture such as one of these:

> *For God so loved the world that He gave His only begotten Son, that whoever believes in Him should not perish but have everlasting life.* (John 3:16)

> *Draw near to God and he will draw near to you.* (James 4:8)

Remember that as you approach God, the things of God will become more prominent.

Recall the words of Hebrews 3:7:

Therefore, as the Holy Spirit says: "Today, if you will

hear His voice," (underline added).

Exercise your will to receive His voice. This involves not only hearing His voice but recognizing it as well.

In this simple activation of the prophetic, you might simply hear God say *"I'm very pleased with you."* Indeed, many in the body of Christ find it difficult to hear these words. Perhaps they did not have a proper relationship with their earthly parents, and so they find it difficult to develop a healthy relationship with their Heavenly Father. Or they could be burdened with a sin-conscious gospel rather than a life-conscious gospel. These are things that the loving Father wants to address in our lives.

Open your heart to hear words of exhortation from the Father who loves you very much. Yes, Father God will speak words of correction sometimes, but I have found after walking with Him for many years using this simple exercise of faith, that it is His desire to love on us. So open your heart and mind now, allowing Him to speak clearly. Recognize His voice and receive encouragement.

At the end of this exercise, you may want to keep your results and practice it again. Regularly applying this exercise and recording your impressions will begin to tune your ear to God's voice. It takes time, practice, and faith. I assure you: **God wants to speak with you today.** This isn't a game. God longs to communicate with His people. He wants you to hear Him. He stands at the door and knocks. His desire to speak to you is greater than your desire to hear Him. So take this time to get quiet and listen for Him, recording and responding to the simple words you hear from Him.

This activation seems simple, but over the years, I have found scores of people who begin to recognize the voice of God through it, opening new doors to strengthen their relationship with Him.

A young man who always felt he had been a failure saw a particular shade of blue: sky-blue. From this, he felt God saying that the sky was the limit for him, and that he needed to step out and become a risk taker. So with just a few thousand dollars, he started a business that became very successful.

When I was born again, I discovered the prophetic way of life. I began to hear things and know things that I had no way of knowing. I realized there was a realm to God that I must discover. I did it in simple ways.

My wife Susan and I would go to the supermarket together, but I would remain in the car and watch people. I can truthfully tell you that I enjoy watching people. The human race is so entertaining! As people came out of the store, I would guess what car was theirs. Sometimes I'd get it right, but most times I'd get it wrong. One day I heard the Lord say: "Ask me which car is theirs." So I began asking God and listening intently. And you know what? I started to get them all right. This was not an easy process, but it taught me to recognize the voice of God. I learned to quit guessing and start asking. Once I did so, my accuracy began to increase.

Father God is relational and wants relationship with you. He wants to partner with you so that when you ask Him with right motives, He will reveal what you ask. It is important to understand that we cannot manipulate God to work on our behalf in areas that are unrighteous and selfish. Had I been in the auto-repo business, I doubt God would have spoken to me like He did in that supermarket parking lot. However, we can partner with Him so that many receive a word from God: a touch from heaven that will draw them unto Him.

Jesus said,

> *"And I, if I am lifted up from the earth, will draw all peoples to Myself"* (John 12:32).

It is very important that we judge the motives of our heart as to why we desire to hear from God.

Many times when I am ministering in the prophetic, I recognize that a person's countenance is low. I ask the Lord why they are struggling and what has caused their hurts. By asking this question and setting my heart to recognize His voice, He begins to reveal the answers.

What did you write on your paper? What did you hear Him say?

Yes, most of the time when you do this exercise, He will speak directly for you, but He may also give you a word for your family, for your friends, or your neighbors. God is continually speaking, but many have never fine-tuned their spiritual ear to recognize His voice.

Is this helping? Are you excited? Is it stirring you? Please know it is the Father's heart to have constant communion with you.

The Second Exercise

Let's look at another activation of the prophetic designed to take us into a deeper realm of prophecy. This will require us to focus on the voice of God in new ways. In this exercise, you will need at least one other person, preferably someone that you are not well acquainted with. Ask them if you can pray for them, and then set your heart to hear from God as you pray.

In the School of the Prophetic, I will ask people to come forward. Then I begin with one person and ask him or her to pray for the person on their left, then ask the person that was prayed for to pray for the person on their left, until all in the circle are prayed for. In doing this, especially when people are not well acquainted, they will literally stand amazed at the accuracy of their prayers.

Now, when I say "pray for the person," I'm not talking about a rote prayer. I am referring to honest, open communication inspired by Holy Spirit to the Father on the person's behalf. It requires a heart focus of the prayer to the pray-ee. I assume the people praying are believers and are at least comfortable being led by Holy Spirit in a simple way. This exercise doesn't work by repeating, *"Our Father, Who art in Heaven..."*

As you seek to become more prophetic, ask others to join you in prophetic activations. Try getting with five people and asking one to step into the middle while the other four ask God to give them something for that person. You may find that each person will get something different, but then all of the words put together will bring forth a much clearer picture of what God is saying.

Caution

1 Corinthians 14:4 teaches that prophecy edifies the church.

When conducting these activations publicly, keep the prophetic prayers and words simple. Stick to scriptures, comforting words, and positive reinforcement. It is not wise to give strong words of direction when you are first learning prophecy. Words that direct someone's life should be avoided. Stay away from direction about marriages, (past, present, and future) winning lottery numbers, gender of unborn children, or selling houses and moving to mission fields. This level of prophecy certainly has a place, but in the public exercise of activating the prophetic, keeping the words simple and edifying leaves less room for error and more freedom for experimentation.

Further, if you are ever given such a life-changing word, be sure to submit that word to your local body, to trusted leaders, and to God BEFORE you act on it. Never step out on the word of another, regardless of their reputation, authority, or your momentary conviction. We are all fallible. Confirm every word to determine what the Lord is saying to you through it. I cannot stress this enough. I have seen lives wrecked because well-meaning people carried out the words of other well-meaning people without first checking with their well-meaning God! And that doesn't begin to include the havoc and destruction from satan's messengers clothed in light. Ultimately, prophecy should lead you to the word of God. Be sure it does.

Third Exercise

Now let's discuss a greater activation that I often use. In this activation, I have 10 people come to the front, turn their backs to the congregation, close their eyes and pray quietly in the spirit. Once this is done, I ask for volunteers, who do not know the people up front, to come and stand directly behind each person. They are to remain quiet, giving nothing away about themselves or their lives. (For example, if a wheezing old man was told that God wanted him to stop smoking, I would suspect something other than a divine connection.)

Once each of the 10 people have someone standing behind them, I pass out a picture, turned face down. Then I give them about 45 seconds to look at the picture and open their heart to Holy Spirit, asking God to give them a word for the person standing behind them, based on anything triggered by the picture.

So what does the picture do for the people who will prophesy? There is nothing magic about it. It is simply for God to trigger a word for the person standing behind them. It opens the door to a suggestion, a hint, a menu of options, helping God jog the fledgling prophet's spirit to receive something for the other person.

After each person prophesies, I ask the person behind them if the word given had any relevance to them. Of course, I expect complete honesty in this. And I can only get it if there is no pressure to perform, and no sense of critical judgment. Failure — if we can call it that — only paves the way for our success. People have to learn what works and what does not, and they can only learn this constructively in a safe environment. In the early stages of prophetic activation, straightforward feedback is essential. Forget the Christian persona of being "a nice person," and give it to them straight. Feedback like "your prophecy did not seem relevant to my life," might be exactly what the young prophet needs to fine-tune his or her spirit. However, over the past 25+ years that I have held activations of the prophetic, I never cease to be amazed at the overall accuracy from people who thought they did not recognize the voice of God.

Fourth Exercise

For this exercise, I stand someone facing a wall with eyes closed and I tell them that I will or will not have someone stand behind them. (Actually, I almost always have someone stand behind them.) After I put a person behind them, I then instruct the person facing the wall to ask the Lord for a word for that person behind them. I have heard extremely accurate words come forth in this exercise.

One such word came to a young man about his future in politics and as a lawyer. It was highly encouraging and very accurate. The person giving the word had no way of knowing who was standing behind them, but the word had a major impact on that young man.

He is currently in law school and planning for his life in politics.

When there is no one standing behind them, it is common for the person at the wall to say that they are receiving nothing. Sometimes they will get a word but indicate that it is for a certain person in the congregation, or for the entire congregation.

Among the Prophets

If prophetic activations are to work, those of us who are mature in the prophetic anointing must play a part in changing the spiritual atmosphere. I love when the dancing hand of God enters a room. When the prophetic becomes activated, the spirit of God manifests, allowing the prophetic revelation in the room to reach a higher level. It is very important to recognize that the environment has changed and can be engaged. The Scriptures record that Saul, who was not a prophet, began to prophesy in the presence of other prophets. He was participating in the spiritual environment.

Conclusion

There are many activations of the prophetic that can be done. You can develop your own. In doing so, prepare your heart to recognize and speak forth in faith what God reveals. Be safe in your experimentation, and be open to God. There is safety in numbers; there is strength in His Body.

Two are better than one,
Because they have a good reward for their labor.
For if they fall, one will lift up his companion.
But woe to him who is alone when he falls,
For he has no one to help him up.
Again, if two lie down together, they will keep warm;
But how can one be warm alone?
Though one may be overpowered by another,
two can withstand him.
And a threefold cord is not quickly broken.

(Ecclesiastes. 4: 9-12)

Further Information

If you seek greater information on activating the prophetic, than what is contained here, please contact me at ClayRNash@AOL. com. I have a team of prophets available for activations for groups and churches.